Praise for *Soul a*

Soul and Destiny *is a clear, grounded, and hugely inspiring guide to finding our way to fulfilling our highest destiny and living our spirit's true potential. Drawing from his significant years of deep work with others, Alan Cohen shares many down-to-earth practical examples of how to put spiritual principles into use in daily life. Anyone who is seeking comfort, confidence, and guidance will find immense riches in this wise and heartfelt guide to living a life of joy, reward, creativity, and connection.*

—Sonia Choquette, *NewYork Times* bestselling author of
The Answer is Simple; Love Yourself...Live Your Spirit

Soul and Destiny *is an empowering map of how to create our life's purpose. Practical tools and expansive ideas will support you on a journey to achieving authentic happiness and a life which is meaningful, fulfilling, and uplifting. This uniquely inspiring book is a must read.*

—Anita Moorjani, *New York Times* bestselling author of
Dying to Be Me and *Sensitive is the New Strong*

With great clarity and wisdom, Alan Cohen has written a practical book about the deepest questions of our soul: Who are we, and what are we here for? Not only will Soul and Destiny *inspire you, it will give you exactly what you need to soar. If you want a joyful, purposeful, and fulfilling life, put this at the top of your reading list. You really can find meaning in your life, and Alan Cohen will show you how.*

—Debra Landwehr Engle, Amazon #1 bestselling author of
The Only Little Prayer You Need

Whenever I read any of Alan Cohen's books, it's as if I'm being transported to a magical campfire, with Alan as the master storyteller, where he is sharing ancient spiritual wisdom, presented in an easy-to-understand way. Soul and Destiny *does exactly this, and it's the perfect compass to help us tune into our soul's guidance, very much needed in what's happening globally right now.*

This wonderful book helps us to listen to Spirit's voice, so we can choose the path that leads us back home, to a light-filled world where we know that we are eternal souls, forever connected with God and with all of life. And as we make this journey back home, we extend this light through us, helping to uplift our world. And the medicine our world needs right now is our light.

—Cissi Williams, Teacher of Energy Medicine, Osteopath, Naturopath, NLP Trainer, and founder of *Let Spirit Lead* podcast.

Soul and Destiny *is such a beautiful and inspiring book. Life is filled with ups and downs, and it's easy to get lost, and forget what's really important. This book is filled with wisdom, and gives me the practical tools I need to find my way home. I will keep it by my bedside and go back to it again and again.*

—Dan Strodl , Editor of *Miracle Worker Magazine*, Manager of Miracle Network

Also by Alan Cohen

Are You as Happy as Your Dog?
A Course in Miracles Made Easy
Dare to Be Yourself
A Deep Breath of Life
A Daily Dose of Sanity
Don't Get Lucky, Get Smart
The Dragon Doesn't Live Here Anymore
Enough Already
The Grace Factor
Handle with Prayer
Happily Even After
Have You Hugged a Monster Today?
I Had It All the Time
How Good Can It Get?
Joy Is My Compass
Lifestyles of the Rich in Spirit
Linden's Last Life
Looking In for Number One
The Master Keys of Healing
My Father's Voice
The Peace That You Seek
Relax into Wealth
Rising in Love
Setting the Seen
Spirit Means Business
The Tao Made Easy
Why Your Life Sucks and What You Can Do About It
Wisdom of the Heart

SOUL
AND
DESTINY

WHY YOU ARE HERE
AND WHAT YOU CAME TO DO

SOUL
AND
DESTINY

WHY YOU ARE HERE
AND WHAT YOU CAME TO DO

ALAN COHEN

ISBN 978-0-910367-05-9

E-book ISBN: 978-910367-15-8

Printed in the United States of America

*In gratitude and celebration for the Universal
Principles that allow every soul to fulfill its
divine destiny and come home to love*

CONTENTS

INTRODUCTION

On August 19, 1939, two twin boys in Ohio were separated at birth and adopted by different families. Both were given the name "James" and called "Jim." They each grew up with an adopted brother named Larry and a dog named Toy. When they reunited at age 39, the twins discovered that they had they had both married twice, first to a woman named Linda, then to a woman named Betty. Both had one son named James Allen or James Allan. Both worked in law enforcement, drove Chevrolets, smoked Salems, preferred Miller Lite, enjoyed math and carpentry but hated spelling, and vacationed at the same three-block long beach in St. Petersburg, Florida.

The uncanny similarities in the lives of the Jim twins raise some provocative questions: How much of your life is the result of choices you make, and how much is orchestrated at a level far deeper than the thinking mind can fathom? Are you in charge of your life, or is a Higher Power directing you? Is your destiny fixed, or can you change it? Who are you really, and what are you here to do?

At a time when the world is quite insane and weird events occur that no one could have predicted, we can use all the clues we can find to help us make sense of the senseless. It would be comforting to know that the people and experiences that show up in our lives are not random and we have a destiny more meaningful than trudging daily to a job we dislike, watching an endless stream of daunting news, and competing for social media likes. At some point the quest for meaning supersedes playing out social roles that leave us hungry. We begin to look inward for answers instead of outward. We seek a thread of purpose that ties our story together. We hope that John Lennon was right when he said, "Everything will be okay in the end. If it's not okay, it's not the end."

This book is a wake-up call for your soul; a reminder that you are here for a mighty and meaningful purpose. Most of us have lost touch with our soul. We have become hypnotized and distracted by the endless errands and obligations of daily life. Yet even as we scramble to and fro, our souls remain alive and intact. While we may measure our success by what we achieve in the outer world, it is our connection to our spirit that determines our happiness. When you live from your soul, life lines up in amazing ways, and miracles occur.

In the pages that follow, we will draw aside the curtain of appearances that makes it seem as if the external world has power over your life, and you are the victim of forces beyond your control. Regardless of the demeaning identities that have been laid over you, you are a masterful being that has set up every encounter and experience for your awakening and healing, and to deliver your unique gifts to a waiting world. You have the power to make choices that lead to your highest destiny, while you simultaneously play out intentions you established in co-creation with God at a level far deeper than the conscious mind understands.

At the outset of the coronavirus pandemic, my partner Dee and I anticipated being home for a long time, so we bought a jigsaw puzzle. While we expected to finish the puzzle in a few days, it was much harder than we thought, and we plugged away at it in spurts for several weeks. Finally all of the pieces were in place except one. We knew the exact shape of the piece and the portion of the picture it contained. But it was nowhere to be found. We searched the tabletop and the box the puzzle came in, to no avail. "Maybe the puzzle came with the piece missing," I suggested.

Then I looked down at my chair in the crack between the cushion and the arm. There, to my happy surprise, I found the crucial piece. I set the piece in place, and the puzzle was finished.

When an unexpected or unexplainable event occurs, we may be tempted to believe that it is due to the manufacturer's error. Maybe the puzzle of life came with a piece missing. But it is not so. Just because a piece is missing does not mean it does not exist. It has simply fallen in a crack in the very chair in which you are sitting. Rather than looking in the obvious outer places, you have to reach down and in to retrieve your answer.

We were not born to search. We were born to find. The thought, "there has to be more to life than the one I have been living" is the first glimmer of light shining through the crack in the doorway that leads out of the dungeon. If you are tired of settling, you need a healthy dose of higher vision to jumpstart your soul. No matter what alleys and byways you have wandered into, your sojourn here has meaning, intention, and impact. Everything happens for a reason. When you step back and see the big picture, you take back the power you have attributed to external sources, and you embrace your divine mission as a co-creator with God.

Our world has arrived at a crucial point in evolution. We stand at the crossroads between fear and love, confusion and clarity, despair and hope, defeat and victory. Each of us must choose the road we will walk. These paths have become exaggerated to such an intense degree that it is impossible to straddle the two or go back and forth. The world is like a train station where two trains are leaving the station headed in different directions a few degrees apart. At the outset of their departure, the trains are close enough that if you wanted to jump from one to the other, you could. But the farther the trains move ahead, the greater the distance between them; at some point it is no longer possible to switch. Belief systems in the world have become so polarized that we must each make a stand for where we wish to go. One track takes us to deeper darkness and separation. The other leads to brilliant light and fulfilling connection. Current events are calling us to decide which train we are on, and ride it faithfully to its destination.

We will all make it home. How long that takes, and how difficult the passage will be, is up to us. There are easier, more direct ways to reach the goal than the dark pictures the world has painted. Let us now discover how to hasten that glorious homecoming.

HONEY,
I SHRUNK MY SOUL

My friend Mike felt irritated by the homeless woman camped out on the street near his apartment house. She was dirty, unkempt, and painful to look at. Disheveled hair, teeth missing, a scar on her cheek, the fortyish woman scowled at passersby. When Mike encountered her on his way to work each day, the two made eye contact and shot each other caustic looks. He wished the woman would just take her shopping cart of shabby possessions and park herself elsewhere.

Then one day Mike realized he had become embroiled in very unfair judgments of this woman. He considered the hardships that must have driven her to such dregs, and his heart opened with compassion. Mike decided he needed to make amends. The next time he saw the woman, he told her, "I need to apologize to you."

She looked at him cautiously.

"I have judged you. You don't deserve that. You have obviously had a rough life. Will you forgive me?"

The woman thought for a moment and nodded. "Yes, I forgive you."

Then something extraordinary happened. "Suddenly the woman's face changed," Mike told me. "She became about twenty years old, her eyes shining and skin soft. The scar on her cheek disappeared and her missing teeth were filled in. She looked radiant—like an angel." A tear formed in the corner of Mike's eye as he recounted this miraculous encounter. "The vision lasted but a few moments, but it was so compelling that it changed my entire life. Now when I start to drop into judgment about someone, I remember that woman's angelic countenance and I try to see the goodness in the person in front of me.

"What do you think happened?" Mike asked me. "How did I see her so differently?"

I told Mike, "You caught a glimpse of that woman's soul. In the world of physical appearances, she was disheveled and unattractive. But her true self was impervious to the hardships that had battered her body. The deepest and realest part of her was pure, youthful, and beautiful, no matter the worldly story line her life had taken."

Likewise, a part of you—and all of us—runs far deeper than the worldly drama we play out. The appearances that keep us and others small and separate, do not reveal who we really are. Our soul is the truest element of our life, the ray of light that is God. To glimpse your soul or that of another person is the blessing of a lifetime. Yet such a revelation need not be relegated to rare mystical moments. The faculty of soul vision can be cultivated so we see ourselves as God created us rather than what the world has made of us.

The Curious Case of the Shrunken Soul

From the moment you entered the world, your magnificent, expansive, eternal spirit was stuffed into a tiny package too small for you. Your inner light was dampened, diminished, and dulled. Then the contraction only intensified. You were given the limiting attributes of being a boy or girl, black or white, an age, religion, race, and nationality. You were taught that you must go into the family business, get grades as good as your annoyingly smart older sister, suffer under the disease that killed your ancestors, and carry the financial hardships that suffocate borrowers in a debtor's economy. As you grew up, you assumed you would have to drag yourself daily to a stifling job, and die at the age most people depart, wearing the gold watch you received at retirement after your soul has been worn down to a mere trickle of the life you once knew.

No greater lies have ever been told—except the most fundamental one:

You were taught that you are a body that has a soul. It is not so. You are a soul that has a body. You have been hypnotized to believe you are stuck within the arbitrary boundary of your skin. You traded your immortal identity for a self-image founded in fear, subject to unnatural laws concocted and maintained by sleeping minds, destined to be burnt to powder or eaten by worms. No wonder so many people are depressed! There was a series of movies entitled, *"Honey, I Shrunk the Kids."* You and I have played leading roles in the metaphysical dramedy, *"Honey, I Shrunk My Soul."*

Yet even while the dream of smallness drones on, your inviolable self remains alive, empowered, and intact. Illusions fostered by mass hypnosis have not daunted your divine identity. During sound sleep, deep meditation, elevated creativity, moments of revelation, or at the time of death, you remember that the real you spans far beyond anything your physical senses can touch. People who have had near-death experiences report that they no longer fear death because they know that their true self could never die.

They are no more trapped in a body than the sky could be contained in a jar.

Even to say, "your soul" is misleading because it implies there is a "you" that has a soul. There is no such "you." The only real you *is* your soul. You are an expression of life individualized to a unique, highly-focused viewing point. As one philosopher stated, "God is a flower that grew a nose to smell itself." While we consider self-consciousness a character deficit, becoming self-conscious is the entire purpose of your existence. But it is not the small self, identified with the body, personality, and social roles you are to become conscious of. It is your true Self, a pure expression of God, as Richard Bach described in *Jonathan Livingston Seagull*, "perfect as an unwritten number, everywhere at once across space and time."

Stuffing your soul into a body is like forcing your foot into a shoe far too small for it. Your foot hurts, you wobble like a drunkard, you develop blisters, and it feels unspeakably good when you take it off. All suffering proceeds from the erroneous belief that you are a body only; that you are separate from all other souls, alone and abandoned, walled off by chunks of decaying flesh. Your soul knows none of these fictions. The soul remembers its eternal connection to God, and delights in your unity with all that lives.

Awakening from Spiritual Amnesia

All of the world's problems can be traced back to spiritual amnesia. When you forget the depth of your true self, you live in the shallows of life, and then wonder why you feel unsatisfied. Your body and intellect are like goldfish swimming at the surface of a vast, unfathomable ocean. Your soul is a whale that plumbs the depths and rules the sea.

A life without soul is but an imitation of life. Fifty million Americans are on mood-altering prescription drugs, mostly for depression, because they have lost contact with their soul. You do not need drugs to escape from depression, although they can help as an interim step. The ultimate cure for depression is expression. You cannot be depressed and expressed at the same time. The only cure for miniscule living is magnitude. Because grandeur is your true nature, as you tap into it, you overcome all sense of feeling stifled. Living from the soul brings life because the soul *is* life.

Psychologists are sometimes called "headshrinkers." If you go to see your "shrink," it is because you have already been shrunken, mostly by dwelling in your head rather than your heart. A true psychologist is an *unshrinker.* The soul can never be shrunken, but we can distance ourselves from the power it offers us. Real psychology is the restoration of the soul. Only when you get your soul back can you live a healthy, productive life.

In the chapters that follow, I will guide you step-by-step to resurrect, restore, and reinstate your soul. The time of playing small and shrinking into the shadows is over. The fact that you have found your way to this book means you are ready. Every soul has an appointed time of awakening, when the old world has become too confining, and you are ready to claim your innate majesty. That time is now. Let us get on with what we are here to do.

THE WORLD IS
YOUR THOUGHTS
PUSHED OUT

I coached a woman named Joan who had been engaged three times, but sadly two of her fiancés died and one disappeared before the couple reached their wedding day. When I explored with her the beliefs she had been taught as a child about men and marriage, she confessed that her father had left her mother when Joan was very young, and her mother repeatedly told her, "Men don't show up."

Was Joan subject to a dark destiny dictated by a punitive God? Or could her early imprinting about men and marriage have determined the matrimonial path she followed? Was she doomed to tragic relationships and a life of loneliness? Or could Joan somehow shift her beliefs so she would attract a man who survived their engagement?

The events you experience are not imposed by an external, impersonal, capricious source. They are the logical culmination of two crucial elements: (1) The intentions you set forth at a soul level; and (2) the thoughts you focus on. This is why it is so important to choose thoughts that represent where you want to go, not what you want to get away from. Every thought is a seed that bears fruit like itself. At this moment you are constructing your destiny with the ideas you are entertaining.

Understanding the crucial relationship between your thoughts and the results they engender is the first step to undoing painful patterns. If you keep attracting unavailable relationship partners; or unexpected expenses snatch money from your hands before you can spend it on things you enjoy; or you feel burdened by a parent who tries to manipulate you with guilt; or you keep reverting to a painful addiction; or you are dealing with a chronic illness you haven't been able to heal—you can transform all of these hurtful patterns by shifting the beliefs that perpetuate them.

Imagine you are playing chess, and every time you move a piece to a new position, it snaps back to where it was. No matter how hard you push and how firmly you hold your hand on the piece in its new place, the moment you release your hand, the piece reverts to its original position.

Then you lift up the piece and discover there is a small magnet on its underside. You examine all the pieces, and they, too, are embedded with magnets. Then you look on the underside of the chess board, where you find a configuration of strong magnets in the precise pattern your pieces keep reverting to. Now you understand why your pieces won't move forward.

The events in your life configure according to the magnet of your mind. What happens on the outside reflects what is happening on the inside. The world is not a cause; it is a mirror. External conditions do not create results any more than a mirror causes a swatch of your hair to be out of place. If you try to fix the unruly hair by rubbing the mirror, it will not move. You must manipulate the source. While we tend to believe life is happening to us, it is happening *from* us. Mind is cause and the world is effect.

Which Came First, the Chicken or the Robot?

French biologist Dr. René Peoc'h conducted a fascinating experiment with profound implications. Dr. Peoc'h hatched a group of chicks and imprinted them on a small cylindrical mobile robot. (Imprinting occurs when an animal sees an animal, person, or object soon after birth and follows that object as if it is its mother.) Dr. Peoc'h placed the robot in a small rectangular arena, where it tooled around randomly like a robo-vacuum that roams around your living room floor. As expected, the robot moved about the entire arena.

Then Dr. Peoc'h placed the chicks in a cage adjacent to one side of the arena. He turned the robot loose again and monitored where it roamed. This time the robot stayed close to the chicks' cage, and did not explore the area at a farther distance from the chicks.

This striking phenomenon implies that the intention of the chicks to keep their "mother" close to them over-rode the robot's program to roam at random. While chicks don't "think" as we do, their desire emitted a strong energy, which drew the object of their desire to them. Translated into human terms, when we broadcast an intention through our thoughts, feelings, attitude, wishes, and expectations, we exert an influence on the universe that draws the object of our desire to us. Some people call this dynamic the Law of Attraction. No matter what we name this phenomenon, the universe responds affirmatively to our thoughts, and the people, things, and events that surround us are a direct result of our intentions. What shows up in our life is not random at all. There is no such thing as luck. There is only thought and its results.

If you are going to make sense of your life and create a positive destiny, you must recognize the implicit connection between your mind and the world you see. Even if you don't believe that your thoughts attract events, you must admit that your thoughts strongly influence your experience. The world is what it is, but your experience depends on what you make of it. I will now show you how to make the world what you want rather than allowing the world to make of you what it wants.

A GUIDED TOUR
OF YOUR MIND

I saw a film about a woman who had served as a spy for the United States Army. She had been stationed in Europe, where she collected data on foreign governments. Upon her return to this country, she visited a highly-secured military installation, where she was taken on a top-secret tour to a sector seventeen stories below ground level. There she was shown wreckage from extraterrestrial spacecraft that our government had collected.

This is not a book about aliens, but it is about crucial data that is stored below the surface of your conscious awareness. Envision your mind as a house with three floors, one at ground level, and two floors below. What goes on beneath the surface exerts far more of an effect on your life than what happens in the obvious sector. Let's take a look at how your mental home is constructed, so you can access the source of your experience and gain maximal power to choose how your life turns out.

Ground Floor: The Monkey Mind. The ground floor entry level to your mental home is the intellect, a survival mechanism that contains all the data you have ever gathered about what is required to sustain your body and its enterprises. This mode of thought is continuously calculating, manipulating, and planning in order to protect and preserve the body, maximize physical pleasure, and minimize pain. The thinking mind notes who and what will further the goals of the body and its initiatives, and who and what threatens them. As a survival tool, it works well.

The intellect is generally scattered and easily distracted. If you could see a graph of where your thoughts roam during the course of a day, you would be appalled at the multitude of directions in which it is pulled like an unruly child that wanders off at the slightest dazzle. Yogis call this the "monkey mind." We classify some people as ADD or ADHD, but we are all drawn in many different directions, often contrary to our deeper intentions. It is a rare person who can marshal laser focus and corral the intellect to become single-minded long enough to create a chosen desirable result.

When the reasoning mind is harnessed for a higher purpose, it yields upliftment, service, and healing. Geniuses and inventors like William Shakespeare, Nikola Tesla, and Steven Jobs sharply focused their thinking mind toward ennobling humanity. When you hire your intellect as your servant instead of letting it run roughshod as your master, you are making the best possible use of your mind. Then your creations are a gift to you and everyone you touch.

Basement Floor: Subconscious beliefs and patterns. On the floor below your thinking mind is the subconscious, the hidden source of the bulk of your experience. The subconscious is primarily emotion-based, storing both blissful and painful memories so you can recognize joyful opportunities and avoid threatening situations. If you had a trauma you have not resolved, the subconscious stores that memory until you address and heal it. While you may believe that your conscious mind is generating your experiences, it is the subconscious that makes most of your decisions. Jesus said, "As a man thinks in his heart, so he is." The operative words in this teaching are "in his heart." In Jesus's time there was no fancy word like "subconscious," which Freud and other psychologists came up with millennia later. Yet our contemporaries are referring to precisely the same apparatus—the deeply imbedded beliefs, below the level of conscious thought, that form the foundation of our experience.

Countless coaching clients have told me, "I have a recurring pattern in my relationships [or finances, career, or health] that I know is due to some unconscious belief I am holding. I recognize that pattern intellectually, but those situations still come up. How can I heal that counterproductive belief that is causing those unwanted experiences?"

Great question! I will answer it in depth in our next chapter. For now, let's simply recognize that there are strong elements that manufacture our experiences from below the surface of our conscious awareness, factors that the spinning intellect does not plumb to. This is why we need to address and reprogram our subconscious in order to create effective, lasting change in our lives.

Foundation Floor: Soul thoughts. At the level below your intellect and subconscious live your soul thoughts. These are the thoughts you think with God. They are not intellectual concepts, but deep, profound knowing. Your soul thoughts are clear, powerful, and loving. They form the core of all that is good in your life, and empower you to uplift the lives you touch. They are the part of your mind that *is* the mind of God, your real mind. Only the thoughts you think with God are true.

Your soul thoughts are infinitely stronger than your intellectual thoughts or your subconscious beliefs. Soul thoughts override mental meanderings and emotional programming. A coaching client told me, "My mother was a lifelong hypochondriac. She imagined many diseases and spent lots of time at doctors' offices. Yet she lived until a healthy 92 years of age. If our thoughts create our experience, and she had so many thoughts of illness, how did she live so long without being really sick?"

I told my client, "The intentions of the soul supersede mental and emotional programming. On a deeper level, your mother intended to live a long life. She might have been gaining life force by complaining about her apparent illnesses. Maybe she got attention, sympathy, or some other ego reward from her hypochondria. We have to look below the level of appearances to understand a soul's true intentions."

Your soul thoughts are aware of your true destiny, always promoting your highest interest. When you have a date with destiny, such as to connect with a significant partner, establish a meaningful career path, or learn from a life-changing teacher, your soul will commandeer the situation to put you in your perfect place with the perfect people at the perfect time. You may have ideas or plans about where you are heading in your life, but your soul has its ideas—really *your* ideas proceeding from your true self. Because your soul is invested with the power of God, it always prevails. You can attempt to thwart or delay it, but nature bats last. If you sense that your soul is guiding you in any endeavor, follow it.

You can recognize your soul thoughts by the sense of wholeness and empowerment they bring. Lesser thoughts keep you spinning in circles and leave you hungry. You can engage your intellect for a lifetime and still wonder what you are doing here. One authentic soul thought will cut through mental and emotional flak and deliver fulfillment that becomes a touchstone for your entire life.

With this blueprint of your mental house, you gain a vantage point that belief in random events does not provide. This map will help you get where you want to go far more quickly and efficiently than trial and error. Now let's explore ways to bring your intellect and subconscious into harmony with the intentions of your soul, so all parts of you are working together for your highest good.

THE
UNSTOPPABLE YOU

Imagine you are commanding a chariot powered by a team of three strong and spirited horses. If all the horses are responding to your orders, you will make swift progress toward your destination. If the horses are distracted and each of them is running in a different direction, your ride will be chaotic and you will not end up where you wish to go. You will be immobilized and your chariot might even overturn.

The key to success in any endeavor is to align your thinking mind, your subconscious, and your soul. When all three minds are focused on the same purpose, you are unstoppable because what God wills must be so. As a divine being, all power in heaven and earth is given unto you.

Integrity is the state in which all the elements of a system are unified toward one goal. The soul will accomplish everything on your behalf if you quit allowing the subservient elements of mind to make your decisions. There was a television commercial in which a woman kept resisting her mother's help. The tag line was, "Mother, please, I'd rather do it myself!" When we superimpose our ego's will over our soul's will, we get mud. Mucky intellectual and subconscious beliefs clog the pipeline of soul expression. Painful experiences serve as metaphysical Drano, purging obstructive beliefs so the cleansing water of spirit can flow. Every life lesson is either an affirmation of alignment, or a process of getting back into it.

Seven Steps from Sub to Super

It is quite possible to shift a painful pattern to a rewarding one. When you have good tools, you will get the job done far more quickly and efficiently than if you have no tools or cheap or broken ones. Let's say, for example, that you have a hard time attracting or sustaining a healthy, happy relationship because as a child you saw your parents fighting constantly, or you were sexually abused. At that painful time your subconscious registered a red flag alert to avoid such situations in the future. You decided, "Marriage is a war zone," or "The opposite sex cannot be trusted." Then you avoided marriage and kept potential partners at an emotional distance. This strategy makes perfect sense to the protective subconscious. But because the subconscious drew its conclusion from limited data—your singular experience in a dysfunctional situation—it is not aware of the many relationships and families where love, respect, mutual support, and joy are the norm. While your subconscious was trying to help you, it was severely shortsighted.

This is where the soul comes to the rescue. The subconscious is emotion-based, while the soul is vision-based. Your soul is not daunted by negative experiences; it parlays them into fuel for spiritual growth. Your higher mind has faith in you and recognizes your potential. It understands that there are lots of trustworthy partners, and many marriages

are harmonious. The subconscious can be helpful to a certain point, but beyond that point its black-and-white edicts
work against you. Your soul, or superconscious, or higher
mind—they're all the same—has the power to free you from
situations that the two lower minds have not been able
to resolve.

Here are seven steps that will help you call forth the
power of your soul:

1. ***Affirm the higher truth.*** An affirmation is a reminder
    of what is already so at the level of soul. The best
    description of an affirmation is, *"The spirit within
    me loves to hear the truth about itself."* A few sincere,
    heartfelt repetitions of a positive affirmation can
    sink into a deep place in your psyche, and serve more
    effectively than a hundred desperate repetitions.
    You might affirm, *"Marriage is a loving relationship in
    which two people come together to support each other and
    create a happy family."* Or, *"There are many good people
    with whom I can build a healthy, loving relationship. I
    open now to connect with a partner who matches my
    highest intentions and well-being."*

2. ***Mobilize prayer power.*** When you pray, you connect
    with the mind and heart of God, Who wants only
    your happiness. You are aligning with the Source of
    all good. If you think that God is a punitive father, you
    will avoid Him. But if you recognize that God is love
    and only love, without gender, you will eagerly turn
    to that Source with trust and positive expectation.
    It's perfectly valid to pray, *"Please show me a way to
    create a happy relationship. I am willing to drop my old
    beliefs that relationships are painful or spouses are ogres.
    Help me attract and sustain a relationship with a healthy
    partner that works magnificently for both of us. I will not
    try to dictate or manage how that happens. I now place*

my relationship journey in the hands of God, and I trust that You can and will guide me to my right place in life."

3. **Quit arguing for your limits.** Every time you go over a past failure, complain about what isn't working, or cast yourself as a victim, you reinforce that experience in your mind and increase the likelihood of repeating it. Rather than emphasizing your limits or losses, think, feel, and speak about your vision of what you want and how good it could get. Become an advocate for your possibilities instead of your problems, and you will accelerate the manifestation of your ideal situation.

4. *Focus on positive role models.* Whatever you are fascinated with, you draw into your experience. You will advance rapidly when you pay attention to people who have succeeded at what you would like to achieve. Instilling the subconscious with fear-based images hasn't worked for you, so you need to take a new approach. When you observe positive role models of good partners and happy marriages, you are feeding the subconscious new images it can use to generate experiences equivalent to the role models you are observing.

5. *Connect with like-minded people who support you.* The company you keep says a lot about your intentions. If you hang out with people who commiserate with each other about their problems, agree on victimization, or throw cold water on your dreams, you will stay stuck in the rut you wish to escape. Instead, get together with people who love and believe in you, and cheerlead you to live your vision. Even one or two truly supportive friends can be a huge asset for you to achieve your cherished goals.

6. ***Get coaching, counseling, or therapy.*** When you are stuck in a negative pattern, it can help to express yourself to a person who will listen and support you, and may offer you helpful tools. This person may be a coach, therapist, or a friend or family member you trust, who will listen attentively and validate you. Attempting to solve problems alone can be difficult because we all have blind spots. Others can see you more accurately and help you gain clarity on what you want and how to get there.

7. ***Keep moving ahead anyway.*** Fear can cause us to freeze and hide out in zones that seem safe but keep us stuck. Affirmation, prayer, and counseling bear fruit when you follow them with action. You have heard, "fake it 'til you make it." But acting with confidence is not faking it. Your empowered self is far closer to the real you than your imagined frailty. We can more accurately say, "faith it 'til you make it." Take baby steps so you can gain confidence as you progress. You can date someone lightly without quickly getting involved sexually or marrying the person before you know them well. In many cases, some action is better than no action. When you move in the direction of your dreams, you demonstrate faith in yourself and the Power that will help you get where you want to go.

The Way Out

If an area of your life is pain-ridden, or you feel like your whole life is a mess, you are suffering because you have allowed your monkey mind or a dysfunctional subconscious program to dictate your experience. In such a case, your only viable option is to let your soul take the driver's wheel. *A Course in Miracles* tells us, "You cannot be your own guide to miracles because it is you who made them necessary." The you that got you into pain is not qualified to get you out. Only your soul self is competent to extricate you from suffering. Turn all burdensome situations over to your higher self with the humble prayer, "Please guide me." Then stunning synchronicities will lift you to higher ground.

If you are wondering whether or not to pursue a material goal, such as that shiny new sports car or a date with that attractive person you met at yoga class, turn the decision over to your higher self. Pray, "If this is good for me, bring it on. If not, I am open to receive the equivalent or better." Then let your soul arrange the perfect result. It knows what you need far better than your ego. When you turn your life over to Higher Power, you are not being possessed or determined by a will greater than you own. The voice of your soul *is* your will.

You set your destiny in motion long before ego emerged. The ego shouts its hollow threats, but your soul is rock solid, untouchable and undefeatable by worldly ups and downs. It will lead you out of unworthiness and into grandeur. The soul mind is the one that taught Mozart how to write operas at age six; enabled Thomas Jefferson to pen the Declaration of Independence at age 33; gave Shakespeare his plays and sonnets; revealed to Einstein the secrets of the atom; bestowed the Beatles with incomparably brilliant songs; and inspires all geniuses to deliver their creations to the world.

Soul genius is not limited to famous people. Your soul's mission is equally important in the grand scheme of life. It will take you from the dark to the light, lift you beyond hurdles, and carry extraordinary gifts to humanity through you.

The Game You were Born to Win

It is altogether possible to reconfigure the magnets beneath your chess board to create wellness in every area of your life. When you tap into your soul, which is founded in love, you supersede the ego, which is founded in fear. Prayer establishes a bridge to wholeness that cuts through the mire the ego spawns, and connects you with the Source of all well-being. God can resolve any mess the ego has made, and set you firmly on higher ground.

All healing is founded in an identity shift. You cease to see yourself as a small, limited, broken body or personality, and you recognize yourself as a perfect, divine, whole soul. The real you cannot be daunted or defeated. Only the mini-self, a puny idea built on a faulty premise, can be turned back. Meanwhile your soul marches on to the high calling of destiny. Place your soul in charge of your life, and all of your chess pieces will snap into their perfect places. Then you will win the game of life because you understand how the playing board is constructed.

WHAT ARE THE
CHANCES?

The eminent Swiss psychologist Carl Jung was conducting a therapy session with a resistant patient who had been hiding behind her intellectual posturing. In spite of Jung's many attempts, he was not able to penetrate her protective veneer. The therapist reasoned that something extraordinary would have to happen to get this woman's attention.

During this session, the patient was telling Jung about a dream she had had the previous night in which someone had given her a piece of expensive jewelry in the form of a golden scarab. At that moment, Jung heard something tapping at the window behind him. He turned, opened the window, and found a scarabaeid beetle, golden in color, trying to make its way into the room. Jung captured the beetle and placed it in the patient's hand, saying, "Here is your scarab." This stunning event punctured the patient's defense and opened the door to successful therapy. Further research revealed that such an insect very rarely appeared in that environment at that time of year.

As a result of this experience, Jung coined the phrase, "synchronicity," or "a meaningful coincidence." Other researchers call this phenomenon "serendipity," "seriality," or "simulpathity." By whatever name we call it, the process is remarkable: Some occurrences are so rare, unlikely, or intimately personal that we must look to a higher design than simply chance to explain them.

A Greater Plan

One evening I was having dinner with my buddy Bruce at a tiny casual restaurant in the beach town of Paia, Maui. The restaurant was crowded that night, and we were required to sit at a picnic table shoulder-to-shoulder with people we did not know. During our conversation, Bruce recalled that when he was a senior in an Oregon high school, he joined a small group of students on an educational tour in Africa. He recounted some of the places he had visited, and the highlights of the trip.

At that moment the woman sitting beside me interrupted Bruce, "Excuse me, I couldn't help but overhear your conversation—I was on that trip with you." After a short discussion, Bruce and the woman agreed that they were indeed in the same group some thirty years earlier. We exchanged email addresses, and a few weeks later the woman sent me a photo of her and Bruce, age 17, standing outside a school bus in a remote African setting with twenty other students.

The chances of such an encounter in such an out-of-the-way place at such a length of time from the original event are infinitesimal. The chances of Bruce and I discussing that particular summer at that moment, with that lady sitting right beside us, makes the meeting even more unlikely. This was indeed a meaningful coincidence.

I have had too many uncanny serendipitous connections to believe that we are pawns in a haphazard universe.

A brilliant Mind orchestrates who we meet, at what moment, and what transpires at the intersection of our pathways. When we open to the richer design for our lives, extraordinary people and events show up to give us faith that we are on track with our destiny.

Spirit Arranges the Details

While sitting in the first row of an airplane cabin, I overheard a conversation between two flight attendants preparing a meal in the galley. This was the first time the two had flown on the same flight crew, and they were getting to know each other. One attendant, a bit younger than the other, asked, "Where did you grow up?"

"In Concord, California."

"How interesting—that's where I grew up too! On what street did you live?"

"Elm Street."

"No way! So did I."

"327 Elm—a white house with brown trim."

"I can't believe it—that's the house I lived in! What room was yours?"

"The first room at the top right of the staircase, overlooking the front yard."

"I shouldn't be surprised. That was my room too."

These two flight attendants had grown up in the same room in the same house at different times. Here they were standing inches apart in an airplane flying over the Pacific Ocean.

You don't have to fuss and sweat to arrange synchronistic events. They do not proceed from rational left brain planning. They issue from a mystical source far beyond our understanding or control. If you are entrenched in figuring everything out and predicting the how, what, and when of your interactions, you will miss the synchronicities life is arranging for you. The universe is one big synchronicity machine. We just get momentary *aha!* glimpses as if such events are exceptions to the natural order. But synchronicity *is* the natural order. It is happening all the time. When you quit trying to micromanage good things happening, and you relax, trust, and watch for miracles, you will find that good things are constantly unfolding in you and around you.

Famous Synchronicities

Here are a handful of documented synchronicities that will leave you scratching your head:

- United States Presidents Thomas Jefferson and John Adams, principle framers of the Declaration of Independence, died hours apart on July 4, 1826—fifty years to the day after the signing of that monumental document. Fifth U.S. President James Monroe died on July 4, 1831.

- John Wilkes Booth, who assassinated President Abraham Lincoln, had a brother Edwin, who, years before the assassination, had been standing on a New Jersey train station platform when a young man near him started to fall off the platform in front of a moving train. Booth grabbed the fellow by the collar and kept him from falling onto the tracks, saving his life. The man he saved was Robert Todd Lincoln, son of Abraham Lincoln.

- Just after Paul Grachen asked the girl he had been dating, Esther, to be his girlfriend, he was paying for a sandwich when he received change including a dollar bill with "Esther" written on it. Thinking this odd, he showed Esther, who was surprised but remained silent. The couple eventually married, and then Esther informed her husband that seven years earlier, after a bad breakup, she had written her name on a dollar bill with the intention that she would marry the man who returned the bill to her.

- While newly-engaged Stephen Lee and his fiancée Helen were paging through some family photographs, they were shocked to find the bride's mother and the groom's father in a photo together. Inquiry revealed that the couple had nearly gotten married in Korea in the 1960's, but did not wed because their parents forbade the union. The star-crossed parents inadvertently ended up sharing grandchildren.

- Aimee Maiden and Nick Wheeler were perusing family photos while planning their wedding. They were stunned to find a photo showing the two of them a few feet apart on a beach, 11 years earlier, around age 10. Their families, who did not know each other, lived 300 miles apart in England, and just happened to be vacationing at the same time and place.

- Ten-year-old Laura Buxton inflated a red balloon and wrote on it the words, "Please return to Laura Buxton," with her address. Then she released it into a strong wind. The balloon was carried 140 miles until it landed in the yard of another 10-year-old girl—named Laura Buxton. The two girls met and found that they looked and dressed alike. They both had chocolate Lab dogs, a grey rabbit, and a guinea pig, which the girls brought to their meeting without any previous discussion.

- While American writer Anne Parrish was on vacation with her husband in Paris in 1920, the two were browsing in a used book store. Anne noticed a book, *Jack Frost and Other Stories,* and commented that she used to own a copy of this book when she was a child; to see it brought back lovely memories. Her husband opened the book and discovered the inscription in his wife's handwriting, "Anne Parrish, 209 N Weber Street, Colorado Springs." This was the very same book Anne owned as a child.

Negative Synchronicities

While we often speak of synchronicities as happy or inspiring occurrences, the dynamic can also apply to painful circumstances. People who are victims of mass shootings, terrorist bombings, airplane crashes, wars, or other disasters had a date with destiny. The string of events that led them to be in that place at that time is no accident. Such individuals appear to be victims from the three-dimensional viewing point only. In the greater picture, there are no victims, only volunteers. Such souls chose to be in that circumstance for reasons known only to them and God. You cannot know the specific reasons for choices others make at a soul level, including the timing of their departure from the physical world. People who perish in odd circumstances may gain a crucial soul lesson or render some service to humanity.

Such a recognition does not excuse or condone hate crimes, mitigate the hardship, or lighten the emotional burden to loved ones who observe a dear one injured or killed. All such events are tragic. Compassion calls us to support anyone in pain for any reason. Yet emotions cannot offset a soul's chosen destiny, which transcends lesser purposes.

In his letter to the Corinthians, Paul noted that "we see through a glass darkly," meaning that our human vision is severely limited. We do not know God's plan for an individual soul or a group of souls. In retrospect, we may get a glimpse of why the event occurred. Such an insight is not the result of mental reasoning, which is not capable of wrapping its cape around divinity. Such insights are given by grace.

Even some dark events indicate that there is far more to what happens than chance would dictate. In 1974, 17-year-old Neville Ebbin was riding his motorbike on the island of Bermuda when a taxi driven by Williard Manders struck him and he was killed. Almost exactly one year later, Neville's 17-year-old brother Erskine was riding on the same motorbike near the same intersection when he was struck by the same taxi driven by the same driver, and killed. Some accounts include a report by the boys' father John Henry Ebbin, stating that the same passenger sat in the taxi on both occurrences.

What could cause such a tragedy to repeat itself? One reason may be that we continue to focus on the original event. When a hardship occurs and we give it ongoing attention through anger, fear, resentment, guilt, or blame, the Law of Attraction tends to bring us more of what we focus on. That scientific law does not "care" what we are focusing on. It simply attracts more of the same. We may not be free to change that law, but we are free to use it in our favor or against ourselves.

This is why campaigns based on "We will never forget" tend to backfire. When you keep posting photos and reminders of a tragedy, you perpetuate the event in the mass psyche and increase its likelihood of recurring in one form or another. This is not to say that we should gloss over cruel experiences, be naïve, overlook injustices, or place ourselves in positions of vulnerability. It is important that we learn from traumatic events and do everything in our power to avoid repeating them. Perhaps the negative event occurred precisely to guide us to make needed changes.

When we continue to harp on the painful event, stir up anger, call for retaliation, and develop an identity around being a victim, we dig a deeper trench. The more we focus on what we don't want, the more we get what we don't want. Instead, we must turn our attention to the desired new result we would like to create, and give that as much attention as possible. When we forgive the perpetrator, we break the chain of karma that may impel the event to recur. Forgiveness does not mean we excuse wrong actions. It means that we take back the power we have attributed to someone else to be the source of our well-being or its lack, and we claim the authority to generate positive, desirable results independent of others' errors. We take charge of our experience instead of letting someone else determine our happiness. Forgiveness is a gift to ourselves more than to the other person. When we find peace of mind, we mobilize the Law of Attraction to send us more peaceful experiences, and extend our well-being to others.

When a negative synchronicity occurs, extract the lesson it offers, pray, and stay in a positive state of mind that will attract positive synchronicity. Even if you have had a string of negative synchronicities, you can change the tide of events by upgrading your consciousness. The Law of Grace supersedes the Law of Attraction. Mercy is greater than mistakes. When you sincerely seek to create a new and better result, a Higher Hand will assist you. We are not required to repeat dire experiences. At every moment we have the power to create a new destiny that transcends our history.

A Course in Miracles tells us that chance plays no part in God's plan. If God is love and only love, and God is good and only good, then all meetings, events, and encounters must be working in our favor. God's plan is too vast for a single intellect to comprehend. When a stunning synchronicity occurs, we get a glimpse of how intricate and brilliant that design is. We can relax and trust that the universe is orchestrating our life with purpose and benign intention.

You cannot force synchronicity, but you can be open to it. An innocent mind finds more blessings than a doubtful mind. "And a child shall lead them" refers not to a physical child, but to the wide-eyed inner child open to miracles. There was a time when you believed life was magical, brimming with wonder and possibilities. Then you were systematically programmed to believe in chaos and externally-imposed fate. Now you are returning to your original innocence. An open mind is the doorway to infinity. Everyone you meet, and all events and encounters are sent by the universe for your awakening and healing. When you accept the gifts laid before you, everything changes.

NOT THE LIFE YOU PLANNED

My friend Marnie was a popular, straight-A high school senior with her sights set on a well-respected college. Her parents feathered her nest and were excited about her becoming the marine biologist she had talked about since her early teens. Then Marnie's unexpected pregnancy rocked her world. After many tears, arguments with her parents and boyfriend, and soul searching, she decided to have the baby whether or not anyone else agreed with her or supported her.

Marnie finished high school, scrapped her plans for college, and married her boyfriend. But there was no substance to the union, and he disappeared within a year. Here she was, age 19, alone with an infant in a small apartment, struggling to support both of them, taking temp jobs she could do from home.

When her daughter was old enough to go to pre-school, Marnie took a job as a veterinary assistant, which she loved. She attended a community college and then got into veterinary school, where she earned her degree over six years. In that school she met a wonderful guy who became the perfect dad to her daughter. The two married the day after they graduated, and set up a clinic in northern California.

Marnie became interested in holistic animal care and became a highly-respected authority in the field. She now enjoys a hugely successful career and loving family, including a son she had with her new husband. Her nightmare gave way to a soul-rewarding outcome even more fulfilling than her original vision. Along the way, she learned valuable lessons in self-reliance, trust, and resilience that she would have not gained had she walked the path she had planned.

Like Marnie, many of us have had unanticipated events propel us in a direction we would never have imagined. Perhaps you fell in love with someone who did not match your soulmate picture, or you had an unplanned baby, or you faced a health challenge, a job loss, a divorce, or a move to an odd location. Or some stirring event showed up out of the blue, like a well-paying job opportunity, an esteemed mentor, or a spiritual epiphany. John Lennon said, "Life is what happens to you while you're busy making other plans."

While it may seem that unexpected bends in the river thwart us, they can powerfully advance us. Even the hard stuff makes our life better as we come to understand its purpose. We can integrate surprises into the greater mosaic of our journey, and turn hardships into miracles.

The small self struggles to plan life, manipulating and controlling to maintain the known world and protect itself from perceived dangers. The higher self, by contrast, flows in recognition of a wiser will. At some point we realize a design grander than the one we planned, and grace stands where karma seemed to rule. Gratitude, curiosity, and anticipation become the only feasible responses to unexpected change.

In my own journey, the best things that have happened have been totally unplanned, way off the radar screen of my life as it was or as I envisioned it. People and events showed up out of nowhere, plot twists that gave way to a surprise destiny. God had a far better idea for me than I had for myself. Here are a few examples:

From the Slums to the Sanctuary

When I was thirteen years old, my family moved to low-income government-subsidized housing, aka "the projects," a horrible inner city neighborhood. Crime and drug abuse were rampant. I was ashamed to bring school friends home because kids in my apartment building regularly urinated in the elevator, which reeked. Someone broke into the community storage room in the building's basement and stole all the possessions my family kept there. The teenage boy next door, I found out, had been abusing a little girl across the street. I hung out in pinball parlors and roamed city streets in my leather jacket. My world was murky and empty; I had no idea how much I was starving for purpose.

My bar mitzvah was a hollow chore. I hated going to Hebrew school and I counted the days until the spectacle would be over. I gritted my teeth through the ritual and the party that followed. The event was meaningful for my parents, but not for me. I swore I would never set foot in the temple again.

A few months later I received a postcard inviting me to the synagogue for a brunch for teens. I had absolutely no reason or desire to return to that torture chamber. But a voice within me said, "Go." I could not believe I was considering this. I now recognize that voice as my soul prompting me to fulfill my destiny.

At the brunch, a young rabbi named Stuie, the temple's youth director, delivered an impassioned speech. As he spoke, something inside me stirred. This inspiring man was the first person I had ever met who had a positive, loving relationship with God. His eyes sparkled and he exuded kindness and caring. Immediately I felt drawn to his energy.

I joined the temple youth group, a far healthier influence on me than the troubled characters that populated my world. Stuie became a loving big brother and positive role model. He saw good in me that no one else in my life elicited. He encouraged me to run for president of the youth group, and before long I was spending my evenings at the temple, and weekends at Stuie's house with other kids from the group. Quickly my life changed; I found my way from a dangerous den to a healthy family. I was giving speeches to the youth group and adults, and leading prayers for the entire temple. I had been plucked out of hell and my feet set on the lawns of heaven.

I adopted Orthodox Judaism as my spiritual path and I observed the very strict rituals. My life revolved around my rabbi big brother, my friends from the temple, and my relationship with God. Stuie later helped me get a scholarship to a Jewish college. Those seven years proved pivotal to my entire future. My invitation to that youth brunch and meeting Stuie was a date with destiny engineered at a level of soul far, far deeper than any plans I was making for myself.

The Book that Wrote Itself through Me

I eventually traded Judaism for a spiritual path rather than a religious one. I grew ravenous for any wisdom that could guide me how to live. I meditated at a remote Zen monastery, sat before Hindu gurus, attended Christian services, put myself in the most challenging yoga postures, and read every book I could get my hands on that might lead to enlightenment. I was a vacuum cleaner for truth.

I rented an attic room in my friend Barbara's house and spent a lot of time studying and praying. Barbara went for a reading with psychic Vincent Ragone, during which she did not mention my name or tell him anything about me. During the reading, Vincent interrupted himself and told her, "Tell Alan to write." I found the advice odd, as I had no interest in writing. I thought he meant I should write more letters to my friends. I filed the suggestion away in a rear compartment of my mind.

A few months later, I awoke to hear an inner voice urging me, "Get up and write." I resisted and tried to go back to sleep. But the voice persisted until I got up and took a seat at a little wooden desk tucked beside an attic window. I took pen to paper and began to jot down some thoughts I might use as a lesson for a yoga class I was teaching. The flood of ideas became more and more intense until my hand could hardly keep up with the current. Long-forgotten experiences started to make sense as I pieced them into the greater tapestry of my journey. Before long the writing took over, as if I was being dictated to, rather than generating the text.

Soon I was writing ten to twelve hours a day, stopping only to eat and take long jogs in the park to ground me. At some point I realized that a book was being birthed through me, a series of essays on love, relationships, healing, and the spiritual path, interspersed with poetic channeled messages. I titled it, *The Dragon Doesn't Live Here Anymore.*

When the book was complete, I showed it to Barbara. She smiled and went to her closet and pulled out the cassette tape recording of her reading with Vincent Ragone. I listened and heard the psychic say something about my writing that Barbara had not told me: "I think a series of poetic essays would be very good." There was obviously a plan here.

The book became a bestseller and changed my life entirely. Before long I was jetting around the globe presenting workshops, interfacing with people from many cultures, and developing meaningful relationships with apprecia-tive readers.

There was never a day or a moment in my life when I planned to write a book. It all happened spontaneously, like a time capsule that popped open when the moment was ripe, or a flower that pierces above the soil when the spring temperature becomes warm. At some level far below my conscious awareness, I had made an agreement to write that book. I have never seen more compelling evidence that our lives are orchestrated at the level of soul.

Just Go

A few years later, I received an invitation to speak at the prestigious Human Unity Conference in Hawaii. Living my entire life in New Jersey until that time, I was excited to get a free ticket and be paid to visit those exotic islands. When I turned to page two of the invitation letter, I was shocked to read that this conference did not pay an honorarium to its speakers, and they expected me to pay for my own flight, hotel, and meals—plus a conference registration fee! I felt insulted. Sponsors paid me substantial speaking fees and covered my travel. I grunted and tossed the letter aside.

To quell my disappointment, I sat and closed my eyes to meditate. During that quiet time I saw the face of a yogi, an older man with a turban, dark leathery skin, a white beard, and twinkling eyes. His presence was kind and comforting as he seemed to hover and bless me, saying, "Just go." When I arose from the meditation, my attitude was changed. I realized that although my personality rebelled, my inner guidance was clearly moving me to attend the conference. I had made a commitment that I would never let money inter-fere with me being true to my guidance. Now I was called to put that vow to the test.

The next day, my friend Betty invited me to a program she was hosting at her home that evening. It was the middle of winter, and her house was an hour's drive away, but again something inside me told me, "Just go." When I arrived, Betty introduced the speaker, who happened to be an organizer of the Human Unity Conference to which I had been invited. He began a slide show introducing the event, and when he got to the third image, my jaw dropped. There was a photo of the yogi who had appeared in my meditation. "This is Sant Kirpal Singh," said the speaker, "the spiritual leader who founded the Human Unity Conference thirteen years ago."

Any doubt I had about going to the conference immediately evaporated. There was no way I wasn't going!

Once in Hawaii, I fell in love with the islands. My host took me for a walk on the beach, where I basked in beauty I had never before experienced. Velvet green mountains jutted majestically out of the calm azure sea. Soft warm waves lapped over my feet. I was welcomed by turtles and dolphins. My heart was at peace. I felt more at home than in any place I ever had been on Earth. I knew why I was drawn there.

A year later I moved to Hawaii, which proved to be one of the richest blessings of my life. The beauty of the environment and the aloha spirit of the people became paramount teachers of the grace of God, which have filtered into my teaching and writing that have rippled out to uplift many lives.

A Little Dog with a Big Soul

After several years in Hawaii, I went to stay at a bed and breakfast owned by a friend—another Barbara—on the Big Island. She also raised Pomeranian dogs. When I woke up one morning, Barbara brought the most adorable little puppy into my room and placed him on the pillow next to me. "Yours," she said with a smile. "His name is Munchie—short for Munchkin."

I was not looking for a dog, but I fell in love with Munchie on the spot. There was no question that he and I were soul-mates. Over the years that followed, Munchie became the best friend of my life. We did everything together. Then a seminar participant told me, "I was so miserable that I prayed to God to just let me wake up as happy as my dog." The phrase rang with me. I realized that although I was happy some of the time, Munchie was happy *all* the time. So I decided to take Munchie as my teacher, and I observed what he did that made him happier than me. I recorded his lessons in a little book, added some cute cartoons, and self-published *Are You as Happy as Your Dog?* I wrote the book mostly for fun, a simple way to honor my beloved mentor and capture big-picture teachings in a pocket-sized format.

To my surprise, the book took on a life of its own and found its way to amazing places. When the Supreme Court of the Bahamas opened its session, someone read from the book as an invocation. A Greek publisher found the book at an expo in Frankfurt and brought me to that glorious country to lecture annually. A seminar sponsor in Mexico read the book and invited me to give workshops in Cancun, where Dee and I stayed at the Four Seasons Hotel, all expenses paid, and we enjoyed personal tours of the spectacular Mayan pyramids and sacred sites.

Then a Japanese woman living in New York asked if I would like the book to be published in Japanese. She sent it to a Japanese publisher, who decided to take a chance on the book. When the book became popular in Japan, a seminar producer invited me to speak there, which has led to many years of teaching in Japan, and groups of Japanese students coming to Hawaii for seminars. I have developed many deeply rewarding relationships with my Japanese students and colleagues, and learned as much from them as they learn from me. I count my Japanese connection as one of the great blessings of my lifetime.

I cite these examples of unexpected shifts in direction to underscore the power of destiny to alter the course of a life. I don't think I was just lucky, or I did anything special to deserve such blessings. To the contrary, for a great deal of my life I was quite asleep. I am amazed by the grace that has cared for me when I was far more shortsighted than my angels. If I did anything at all, it was to listen to guidance, act on it, and trust that my step ahead would work. Even amidst our dense humanity, God finds us where we stand and compassionately guides us to our higher good.

A Harsher Change of Plans

Sometimes unplanned dates with destiny come in ways not so gentle or easy. Painful situations show up that force us to change direction. Yet even here are opportunities. Every experience can lead to something better if we are willing to let a greater plan unfold.

Elizabeth Gilbert went through a gut-wrenching divorce that motivated her to travel around the world on a quest to find herself. She chronicled her journey in her book, *Eat, Pray, Love*, which became an international mega-bestseller and hit movie, and propelled her into a life far brighter than she had ever known or imagined.

My friend Jon Mundy was at one time a Methodist minister who became interested in *A Course in Miracles*. As Jon's passion for the Course intensified, he incorporated more and more of its principles into his weekly sermons. Meanwhile, a number of his congregants grew hot under the collar because the Course teachings didn't match their religious views. Eventually Jon was fired. But this radical change gave him the time and inspiration to immerse himself in the Course and develop an entirely new vocation around it. Jon has since published ten popular books on *A Course in Miracles* and he is a sought-after speaker. Now his outer life is in harmony with his inner truth.

Steve Jobs found his college study of physics and philosophy unsatisfying, so he dropped out and enrolled in a Calligraphy course. Little did he know that studying serif and sans-serif typefaces would be the creative platform from which he developed Apple Computers. We are all well aware of the astounding inventions his career path led to, which have revolutionized how we all communicate and work. Had Jobs stayed in his college curriculum, the world may have missed out on some of the greatest technological advances in history.

Jeff Bezos was born to a teen mom who married during pregnancy and then divorced her husband when Jeff was seventeen months old. Three years later, Jeff's mom married a Cuban man who knew only one English word: "hamburger"; he went on to adopt Jeff. Despite a rocky family start, Bezos went on to found Amazon.com and become the wealthiest person in the world, his net worth currently at 160 billion dollars. Steve Jobs and Larry Ellison, billionaire founder of Oracle, were also adopted, which may have stimulated them to carve their unique paths to mega-success.

Falling down can be a powerful prelude to a significant step forward. The only thing more important than what happens to us is what we make of it. Bumps and knocks can change our trajectory so we end up in a place far more wonderful than where we thought we were headed.

The Deepest Plan

The people I mentioned above faced unplanned hardships that catapulted them to fantastic material success. Yet many people take an unforecast turn that does not usher them to material riches, but instead to healing of the mind, heart, and soul—the most important success of all.

I used to correspond with a fellow named Jack who had been incarcerated for many years for selling marijuana. Jack decided to use his prison time for spiritual growth. He read lots of uplifting books, practiced *A Course in Miracles,* and corresponded with people of spiritual intent.

One day Jack learned that the person who had turned him in to the police, had gotten in trouble himself, and he was scheduled to be imprisoned in the cell next to Jack. While waiting, Jack did a great deal of soul searching to get beyond the anger he felt toward this fellow for squealing on him. Finally he was able to tap into his heart to find genuine forgiveness. "I am free at last," Jack wrote to me.

The other man ultimately did not arrive at the designated cell, but Jack made a major spiritual stride in his life, from fear and resentment to love and acceptance. My teacher used to say, "Take what you have and make what you want." If you have made a mistake or something shows up that painfully forces your life in a new direction, you can make that change work in your favor by extracting the spiritual insight it offers. There is always a gift on the other side of the hardship.

When events in the outer world take an unplanned twist, they can untwist us spiritually. What seems to be going sideways is really going forward. The plans of the ego keep us gyrating in circles, a dot endlessly bouncing around on a two-dimensional plane. The soul functions in a far broader dimension. The purpose of our spiritual journey is to become aware of more dimensions than we thought were available. Every event is leading to this glorious realization, including surprises that lead us to lands that fear cannot comprehend and illusions cannot surpass.

Join the Conspiracy

The word "conspiracy" means "to breathe together." Many elements of the universe are breathing together to support you to fulfill your destiny. Spiritual mastery requires a kind of reverse paranoia. A paranoiac believes that unseen forces are plotting to hurt or kill him or her. A person of faith believes that unseen forces are plotting to help and heal him or her. Albert Einstein suggested that there is one fundamental question we must answer: "Is the universe a friendly place?" The Greek word "metanoia" means "transformation of the mind." When you become a "metanoic," you trust that there are cogs and wheels operating behind the scenes to support you to achieve your destiny and help others fulfill theirs.

The fact that most people do not end up living the life they planned is a blessing because the life that most people plan for themselves is far smaller than the life that God has planned for them. The ego's plan is unaware of the soul's plan, the only one that really counts. Even if you have not achieved your material goals, if you have grown spiritually and learned to open your mind and heart to greater truth, your life is a resounding success. When we step aside and let life lay its gifts at our door, we are humbled to recognize that love walks with us always.

THE COSMIC
THEME PARK

When I visited Disneyland, I found a colorful array of realms to enter: Adventureland, Main Street USA, Critter Country, Frontierland, Fantasyland, and Galaxy's Edge, among others. You and I have the same choices in the theme park of daily life. We have adventures, we interact with all kinds of critters, we indulge fantasies, and we must choose whether we will stay on Main Street or explore new frontiers—maybe even poke beyond the galaxy's edge. You don't need to read lots of metaphysical books to discover the options for your life. Just spend a day at Disneyland and take notes.

The world is an extravagant theme park in which every soul has chosen a principle it came to master. If you scan your life, you will recognize that one area has grabbed your attention more sharply than others. You may be focused on issues of physical health, prosperity, relationships, creative self-expression, or your spiritual path. More specifically, you might be learning self-acceptance, authenticity, clear communication, trust in your process, taking back the power you have attributed to others, learning to harmonize with a relationship partner, setting healthy boundaries, or choosing love over fear. This arena of intense focus forms the template upon which you learn and grow.

Your theme is the one that yields the greatest joy and also poses the greatest challenges. It is exaggerated in your experience so you can explore it from many angles and learn its lessons most effectively. Contrast underscores polarities and helps you make strong choices. While you may feel daunted by the difficulties your theme presents, mastering them will yield far more soul growth than the elements of your life that are less pronounced.

You can identify your theme by recurring patterns, such as, "I keep attracting dependent personalities"; or "people don't acknowledge me"; or "authority figures try to control me." You will not end that pattern by avoiding relationships, trying to get more attention, or arguing with your boss. You will end that pattern by graduating from the limiting beliefs that keep the pattern in force. You will look at the underside of the chess board and discover the layout of the magnets keeping the pieces on top of the board snapping back to their original positions. Instead of complaining about narcissistic men, manipulative women, or unfair governments, appreciate those situations as key opportunities for you to master your theme by healing the fears and illusions that have made the pattern a problem.

You can reframe the challenges of your theme as your most valuable learning opportunities. My coaching client Frieda told me, "At 82 years of age, I am still struggling with finances, the biggest bugaboo of my life." I suggested, "Maybe your biggest bugaboo is really your path of highest education. As you get clearer on your money issues, you are mastering the most important lesson of your life." Frieda told me, "I love that angle! I am conquering the monster and doing what I came to do."

So are we all doing what we came to do. Don't worry about figuring out what your theme lessons are. They will find you; they already have. Just live your life as proficiently as you can, and your theme's joys and difficulties will speak to you. Your curriculum has been set at a far deeper level than surface appearances indicate.

One Way or Another

Many people regret the choices they made, and worry about failing to fulfill their destiny. You may be afraid you blew your opportunity to connect with your perfect soul-mate, or you chose the wrong career, or you are living in an inferior place because you can't manifest your dream location. You might blame yourself for poor choices that keep you from your calling, or believe that some external force has thwarted you.

You don't have to fret about such missteps. All beliefs in missing something are distractions and illusions. You are on your path, even when you seem to have wandered. Apparent missteps are a part of the dance. *A Course in Miracles* tells us that in any situation in which you believe something is missing, what is missing is what you are not giving. Don't be seduced into believing there is some space in the outer world that you have failed to fill, or will not fill. You are not cursed with an inner black hole. Everything you need has been given or is available. The universe will keep presenting you with the perfect opportunities to explore and master your theme, one way or another.

If, for example, you can't find a mate who matches you, the problem is not a lack of compatible partners. The problem is that you hold a belief in insufficient supply; or you have fears or resistance to a committed relationship; or you do not recognize your worthiness to have a present, dependable partner. Everyone who shows up and then falls short of your hopes is your teacher pointing you to face your sense of unworthiness or belief in lack. While the process of facing your shadow self may feel scary or overwhelming, when you hold that negative belief up to the light, you will realize it is utterly untrue, even ridiculous, and it will dissolve. You are created in the image and likeness of a perfect, radiant, magnificent God; you are completely lovable; you deserve a partner who adores you and is thrilled and honored to be with you; and there are plenty of people out there with whom you could enjoy a deeply rewarding connection. That's the lesson that all of your relationship "failures" are leading to. But they are not really failures because each experience has brought you closer to the realization of your utter worthiness and the universe's ability to supply what is right and good for you.

Whether one relationship partner hasn't matched you, or a hundred, it does not matter. You will keep meeting people who stimulate you to change your mind about what's wrong, and let love in. Central casting can send an unlimited number of actors to play out the script you have written, until you choose a new script. Everyone you have ever dated, married, divorced, worked with, or observed in a great or horrible relationship is an agent for your awakening. So it is with anyone you stand behind in the line at the post office, the tech support agent who answers your call, or a friend asking for a ride to the airport. You will keep encountering all the right learning partners, whether you live in downtown L.A. or a wooden shack atop the Himalayas. Geography and social conditions cannot thwart your destiny. Everyone and everything you need will find you wherever you are to help you accomplish your mission.

The Man behind the Curtain

Is it really necessary to become aware of the dark places in your mind that are causing you pain? Can't you just focus on the good, immerse yourself in your positive vision, and keep moving ahead? Certainly, the more you focus on the good, the more good you will attract. But if a challenging theme-related situation persists, you must figure out how to deal with it. You must shine light on it until it is resolved. If you get a flat tire while driving, you can't just overlook it and keep driving. You must address the flat and fix it. Yet there is far more to the flat than meets the eye. It's not just a nuisance or delay. You might enjoy being outside and getting some exercise changing the tire after sitting at your computer all day. You might call for roadside assistance, and while you are waiting, watch a YouTube video on your phone that changes your life. You might phone a dear friend you haven't spoken to in a long time, and renew a meaningful relationship. You might enjoy an amazing connection with the repair truck driver when he arrives, or be kind to him in a way that changes his day. You might be grateful that the incident called your attention to an old bald tire, so you can replace it before you have a blowout on the freeway. You might realize that you don't want to keep fixing your older car, and decide it's time to get a new one. There are endless possible blessings that might accrue from a simple event that seems like a waste of time, but yields benefits you never imagined. The mundane but veils the magnificent.

When you become aware of a pattern that has been hampering you, it begins to lose its power over you. I used to start relationships with women who lived far away, and then complain that they weren't available. Then I realized that *I* wasn't available. I chose long-distance relationships because I didn't want to have to deal with the challenges of being with an intimate partner on a day-to-day basis. When I got tired of that pattern and realized that I had been choosing it, I became free to make a different choice. Then I met someone who lived close to me, with whom I have developed a rewarding long-term relationship. The outer is a perfect mirror of the inner.

Illusions hide in the subconscious, where they control your life with concealed dials and levers, like the wizard who intimidated the people of Oz with a smoke-and-mirrors machine hidden behind a curtain. No illusion can stand the light of truth. There's always some little dog that scampers behind the curtain, draws it aside, and reveals the fake conjurer to whom you have attributed magical powers. Now you can take back your power and, like the beleaguered voyager Dorothy, realize you have always had all you need to find your way home. When you sincerely, fearlessly pull the covers off the illusions that have been hampering you, they dissipate into the nothingness they are.

The Path of Least Resistance

The form through which the agents of your theme show up is less important than its essence. Spirit can work through endless and surprising vehicles to help you awaken. I used to consult with a clairvoyant who gave me extraordinarily helpful insights. She once told me, "Soon you will have a son who will help you accomplish the final opening of your heart."

The predication puzzled me, as I was not in a relationship at the time and I was not looking to have a child. I just filed the suggestion away in my mind in the "maybe wrong, maybe later, maybe not for me" drawer.

Not long afterward, my friend Barbara gave me puppy Munchie, who I loved more than words can express. He was like a son to me. Looking back now, I realize the clairvoyant was not talking about a human child. I learned many lessons with Munchie similar to those a father would learn with a human child, including the opening of my heart. My theme found me through the path of least resistance.

A similar dynamic occurs with mothers or couples who want a child, but have been unable to bear one. While they believe they must have a biological child, there are many other ways to experience the joys and lessons of parenting. Couples or singles can adopt, take in a foster child, volunteer at a school or youth center, participate in a big brother/ big sister program, or connect with children in some other creative way. Relationships occur between souls, not bodies. You can have a supremely rewarding relationship with a soul regardless of how that body emerged into form.

Some people birth artistic creations rather than biological children; that is also a valid form of parenting. What comes forth from your soul is your child, whether it is a person, pet, book, art piece, musical composition, house design, course you teach, garden, or any other unique expression that springs from your spirit. Then that creation ripples out into the world and, like a human child, has a life of its own.

Very often couples who adopt because they have been unable to conceive, go on to have a biological child. Here the Law of Attraction shows up in full splendor. When the couple becomes a vibrational match to parenting through an adopted child, that match manifests itself in birthing a biological child. All of life is about frequency, attention, and consciousness.

Missteps become Steps

A few years ago Dee and I were planning a vacation of a scenic train ride through the Canadian Rockies, which ended up in Calgary. Then we had an argument, and to relieve tension I went for a ride in our car. While driving, I noticed that Dee had set the radio on a station we usually didn't listen to. To my delight, I heard a song by the Moody Blues, my favorite band. After the song, the DJ announced that the group would be on tour in Canada, with a performance in Calgary on the very night we were already scheduled to arrive in that city. I immediately booked tickets for the concert, which turned out to be the icing on the cake of a memorable vacation. What started out as an argument led to a marvelous serendipity we both enjoyed.

A GPS provides a perfect metaphor for how we stay on track with our theme. At the beginning of your trip, you program the GPS to guide you to your chosen destination. Along the way, the GPS instructs you, "Turn left here." If you miss the turn or for some reason choose not to take it, the system recalibrates to guide you to your destination via an alternate route. You can miss or resist guidance, but if you do, there is another way to get where you need to go.

Sometimes I hike up a stream in the mountains to get to a hidden waterfall. The stream is strewn with thousands of boulders and small rocks I hop along. I used to wonder if I was taking the best route, choosing the easiest and safest rocks to navigate. My mind was stuck in the "one right way to get there" mentality. Then one day I realized that there are an infinite number of combinations of rocks I could step on that would lead me to the same right place.

Many people get trapped in the "one right way to get there" mode of thought. They fear they might not find the one right way, and fail. Or they think their path to the mountaintop is the only way, and everyone else is wrong. Lots of us labor under a "black or white" mindset. But the universe is far more variegated and gracious. The squares on the playing board are multi-colored. You don't have a choice about where you will end up; you will achieve enlightenment sooner or later. But you do have a choice about the route you will take. Relax and take the path that feels best for you, and don't worry that you will become altogether lost. You may get sidetracked or take some detours, but even those byways are a part of the greater journey.

One of our dogs loves to play tug-of-war. He goes to a huge pile of dog toys in the corner of our living room and chooses one for the contest. Some days he takes his choice very seriously, sniffing many different toys to decide which one he wants to play with today. There is a long purple caterpillar, a thin green alien, and a small yellow chicken. I tell him, "Just pick any one. We will have fun no matter which one you choose."

We humans likewise labor over small choices as if they have cosmic significance, such as whether or not to buy the tan couch or the green one. In the big picture, it doesn't matter that much. What matters is our state of mind while we are choosing. If you are balled up, anxious, and fearful, you've made the wrong choice. The real choice is not the couch, but the consciousness. If you get into an argument with your spouse over tan or green, you have missed the point of the choice. Your soul's theme has nothing to do with the color of the couch, and everything to do with the color of your aura.

Ultimately all life themes can be boiled down to a few simple choices: love or fear; wholeness or brokenness; connection or separation; trust or mistrust. We get distracted by thinking that our choices are between objects, while they are really between states of mind. The spiritual teacher

Bashar states, "Circumstances do not matter. Only state of being matters." When we learn to maintain a peaceful, joyful state of being, no matter what appearances indicate or the state of being others choose for themselves, we are well on our way to master the principle we came to learn.

Transfer of Learning from One Theme to Another

If you are having difficulty gaining the lessons of one theme, you can apply the lessons you have gained from another theme. Most people do well in certain areas of life while they have a hard time with others. We all have a blind spot that keeps us from seeing some aspects of our life clearly. You may be successful in business, but struggle with relationships. Or you may be physically healthy, but feel blocked in creativity. Perhaps you are content to be alone, but you feel anxious in crowds. If so, you can take what you know about what works in your area of expertise, and apply it to the area you are struggling with.

I was coaching a woman who had a successful entrepreneurial business, but couldn't click with a romantic partner. I asked her, "What would you say are the three most important skills that make your business work?"

She thought for a moment and replied, "Being authentic, communicating clearly, and supporting my customers."

"What would happen if you used those same skills in your intimate relationships?"

She looked stunned, and then lit up. "I think they would work much better."

The principles that make life work are universal. They work in *all* areas of life, in *all* themes of learning, *all* the time. You might believe, "Universal principles work well when I see my clients, but when it comes to healing my body, that's a different story." But truth does not make exceptions. Truth is consistent, else truth it would not be. We rope off certain areas of our life as if they are exempt from functional dynamics, and then we suffer. If we would trust that what works here will also work there, there would become as fulfilling as here.

In worldly theme parks, the rides take you in circles. In the cosmos, the rides move you forward on a continuum of awakening. Exploring your theme is like majoring in one subject in college. While you take many different courses, a core curriculum prepares you for your chosen vocation. As a spiritual being, your vocation is enlightenment. Every class in every course is in the service of your illumination. When you complete the ride, you will recognize that you have lived in the Magic Kingdom all the while.

SOUL CONTRACTS

When Dee was growing up, her mom didn't want a dog in the house. Bev thought dogs were dirty, and she didn't want to clean up after them. Years later, when Bev visited us, she fell in love with our little Maltese, Nani. "I would like a dog like Nani," she declared. "White fur, loyal, and a tail-wagger." Dee and I liked Bev's idea, as her husband had passed away, she was living alone, and she would benefit from youthful, vital energy in her home.

A few months later, a dog that perfectly matched that description showed up on Bev's doorstep. He was a friendly white Bichon Frise, tail wagging, eager to play. The dog looked as if he had been groomed, so Bev assumed he was lost. She posted signs around the neighborhood, and no one answered. She took the pooch in, fell in love with him, and named him "Buddy."

A week later, to her dismay, Bev received a phone call from a neighbor couple who had been on vacation. When they came home, they discovered their dog was missing. A short conversation revealed that Buddy was indeed their pet. An hour later, the wife came to Bev's house to retrieve the dog, which broke Bev's heart, but she knew it was the right thing to give him back.

When the woman arrived, Buddy jumped onto the couch beside Bev and refused to budge. The woman called him repeatedly and tried to cajole him, but he wouldn't move. Buddy obviously wanted to stay with his new friend. The woman said she would go home and discuss the situation with her husband. Later that evening she phoned Bev and told her, "The dog really wants to be with you, so you can keep him."

Buddy went on to be Bev's loyal companion for the remaining five years of her life, during which he brought her unspeakable joy. We were stunned when Bev told us that Buddy was sleeping in bed with her and she was feeding him from her own plate with a fork! A radical shift by a woman who at one time didn't even want a dog in the house! But love has a way to soften judgment and pierce to the heart.

After Bev passed, Dee and I could not bear to think of Buddy going to a home that might treat him any less kindly than he had treated Bev. So, even though we already had five dogs, we took Buddy into our family, where he has lived well for seven happy years now.

Agreements at the Level of Soul

Bev and Buddy had a soul contract, an agreement made at a very deep level between two individuals who choose to be together to help each other. Before you were born, you entered into soul contracts to set up your most meaningful relationships with romantic partners, family members, friends, spiritual teachers and students, co-workers, neighbors, pets, and anyone whose life significantly impacts yours. Everyone you interact with, from your high school sports coach, to someone you date briefly, to the person you marry and have a family with, comes by divine appointment.

When we recognize the perfection of all interactions, we understand that everyone comes to us bearing a gift that furthers our soul's advancement.

There are two kinds of soul contracts: The first is with people who love, support, and empower you. They are dear friends and family members who believe in you and exert a positive influence on your spiritual journey. They are your best friend as a child; a grandparent who loved you unconditionally; the teacher who fanned the flame of your talent; your child who elicits profound joy; your esteemed mentor; and the influential leader whose model motivates you to strive to succeed and contribute. Some soul contract partners intersect our life for a key moment, others walk with us for a season, and others bond with us for a lifetime. When you consider the people who have helped you the most, you can be sure you have a soul contract with them.

You also have soul contracts with people who challenge you: an abusive, alcoholic, mentally ill, or absent parent; a schoolyard bully; a spouse who hurts or leaves you; a friend who betrays you; a child you cannot control; a harsh supervisor; a business colleague who cheats you; a disrespectful neighbor; or a despotic, self-serving political leader. While such people appear to be devils, they are really angels. You may feel like a victim to those people or the situations they engender, but you have "hired" them to help you awaken. You might be tempted to curse, resist, or fight them, but as you recognize the gifts they bring, you can bless them. They are truly your friends. When the play is over, the heroes and the villains take their bows, step offstage, retire to the dressing room, remove their costumes and makeup, laugh, and sip wine as they applaud the success of the performance they have achieved together.

Some soul contract partners simultaneously love and support you, and drive you crazy. If they do both, you can be sure you shook hands before you came into the world. In this case, you gain the blessings of their kindness and you must also dig into your soul to find the strength to deal with their challenges. "Love-hate relationships" teach us to maximize the love and eliminate the hate. When you can maintain your inner peace in situations that once disturbed you, you have graduated from your soul contract with honors.

Your Role to Help Others

You also play out soul contracts with people you serve as a hero or villain. Just as you have chosen other people to help you master your theme of learning, others have chosen you to help them master theirs. When you help someone who is troubled, stand by their side during a tough time, or extend grace, you are a vehicle for blessing. We have no greater purpose than to make each other's lives easier.

If your actions challenge another person, you give them an opportunity to learn and grow. While you would not hurt anyone intentionally, if you make errors that disturb them or do things that rattle their cage, they have a choice as to how they will process that experience. Some will be upset, and others will forgive you. Some will berate you, and others will thank you. Such individuals are not victims of you. Your actions stimulate them to choose love over fear, peace over disturbance, connection over separation. Whether they know it or not, like it or not, you are their learning partner.

While sitting on an airplane on my way to meet a spiritual teacher, I was eating an apple. After a few bites, the fellow sitting next to me pushed away, grunted, and made a scowling face. To my embarrassment, I realized that as I was biting the apple, I was squirting him with the juice. When I recognized my error, I stopped eating and apologized. The man refused my apology, groaned, and turned away. For the rest of the flight I felt foolish for unknowingly disturbing my seat partner.

When I met with my teacher, I recounted the experience. He asked me, "Do you see how you helped that fellow?" No, I replied. "That man probably has a belief, 'I always sit next to some annoying person on an airplane.' He attracted you because of his belief; you are an actor in the play he scripted. That fellow will have to keep facing the manifestation of his belief until he confronts it and chooses to forgive the people who annoy him, or he decides that he can attract more pleasant seatmates. While you had your lesson as the squirting apple eater, he had his own lesson. You were perfectly matched to help each other learn and grow."

The same dynamic applies to every interaction in which someone feels disturbed by you. While we must not be lazy or irresponsible about our actions that bother others, or put up with ongoing nuisances, we must recognize that everything happens for a spiritual reason. When we understand the reason, the experience makes sense and we can ascend to the next level of our journey.

Soul Contract Fulfillment Agents

A soul contract may keep uniting you with the person with whom you have the agreement, or someone similar, until the contract is fulfilled. In college I dated a co-ed named Ellen for a while, and then we drifted apart. One day I received a voicemail message from Ellen's roommate telling me that Ellen wanted me to call her. When I did, we rekindled our relationship and went on to be together for four more years. Ellen later told me that she never asked her roommate to phone me. Her roommate knew that Ellen still liked me, and she was playing Cupid. In that case, Ellen's roommate was the channel through which my soul contract with Ellen was fulfilled.

I know of a couple who, after dating for a while, grew irritated with each other and argued. They decided to end their exclusive commitment and see other people. Both went to an online dating service, used alias names, and each found someone they liked. They struck up engaging conversations, and their respective new relationships heated up. Finally they each made a date with their new love interest. When they went to the date, they discovered that their "new" partners were each other!

In Jiang Province, China, 80-year-old Xu Weifang saved an eight-year-old boy from drowning. This was especially admirable in light of Xu's advanced age and the injuries he was nursing. Astoundingly, Xu discovered that 30 years earlier he had saved the boy's father from drowning, as well. Mr. Weifang obviously had a soul contract with that family as their guardian angel!

You, too, have people who serve as your guardian angels to fulfill important agreements, and you serve as a guardian angel through which others can fulfill their destiny. Such relationships are meant to be, for your mutual good. While you may try to leave, cosmic glue keeps pulling you together until you both master the lessons of the relationship. We are connected in amazing ways that help us do what we came to do and aid others to complete their mission.

Group Soul Contracts

Everyone connected to a situation, including delightful ones and challenging ones, has a soul contract with everyone else in that situation for a shared learning. I often coach people who have gotten a divorce or are considering one, and they fear that their children will be negatively impacted. While I do not encourage divorce without significant prayer, forethought, communication, and counseling, if a client has decided on divorce, I explain that their children have their own learning curve related to the divorce. The kids have a soul contract with their parents, who provide valuable lessons and opportunities for everyone to grow. If the child sees parents who love and support each other, with or without a divorce, the child gains a positive role model of relationship. People who divorce with kindness and mutual respect exert a far more empowering influence on children than couples who live together but silently loathe each other, treat each other unkindly, and retreat to private lives. Even amidst rocky divorces, the children must dig inside themselves to make sense of the situation and grow through it. The children may learn that bitterness and hostility don't work, and efforts toward harmony succeed. If the parents part and live different lifestyles, the children will observe the pros and cons of each style and incorporate those observations into their own choices at later crucial crossroads. Processed wisely, the children will take the best and leave the rest.

My client Tom had two fathers: his biological father and his stepfather. Tom's natural father was a flamboyant personality; he gambled, drank, partied, laughed a lot, traveled, and had girlfriends, all of which led to his wife divorcing him. Tom's stepfather was the opposite in every way: quiet, withdrawn, serious, conservative, and controlling. While as a boy Tom was initially confused by the huge disparity in his fathers' personalities and lifestyles, as he grew older, he learned from both of them. "From my natural father I learned generosity, expansiveness, fun, and the willingness to take risks and explore life. Yet my father's extremes taught me to exercise moderation and to respect the feelings of others, which he often didn't do. My stepfather showed me the value of stability and commitment, and to be satisfied with what I have. But he was so serious, almost morose, that I decided I would never dig myself into a dark hole like he did. Ultimately, I learned from both of my fathers what works and what doesn't work. Now that I am grown and I have my own family, I am doing my best to incorporate the positive aspects of each father and minimize the negative ones."

Tom's mother and both fathers had their own soul lessons that interwove with all the other family members. His mother learned from her husbands' contrasting personalities, and they had to figure out how to deal with her and their son. While at first glance the scenario seemed a hodgepodge of divergent personalities and intentions, there was perfection in the opportunities for soul growth for everyone involved. So it is for all family, social, and business relationships.

Soul Contracts with Situations and Institutions

We also have soul contracts with situations, conditions, and institutions. Dealing with a health challenge, for example, can move us to develop character qualities such as patience, perseverance, trust, willingness to accept help, identifying healing strategies we value, awakening to our spiritual identity, and deepening our relationship with Higher Power. The ego judges a health issue as a setback, but if the person is growing spiritually, there is significant soul achievement.

Some people leverage a health challenge to achieve extraordinary spiritual growth and serve as an inspiring model for those who observe them. Franklin D. Roosevelt was immobilized due to polio he contracted at age 39. But being confined to a wheelchair didn't stop Roosevelt from being elected to an unprecedented four terms as President of the United States and ably guiding the country through the Great Depression and World War II. Stephen Hawking suffered from debilitating amyotrophic lateral sclerosis, but claimed his place as one of the most respected physicists of all time. Hawking proved beyond a doubt that the mind is free, independent of the condition of the body. Spiritual teacher Ram Dass had a serious stroke which impaired his speech and mobility. He regained his speech and did not allow his physical deficiency to dampen his spirit. He remained the same loving, compassionate world-class teacher he had been before his stroke. Each of these esteemed leaders used their physical condition as a fulcrum to demonstrate that the spirit soars beyond the physical.

You might also have a soul contract with an institution or a government. A woman who grew up in Communist Russia described the oppressive way the government forced citizens to voice the party line, and punished those who did not. Communism leveraged guilt bigtime to serve its own ends. Her description reminded me of religions and cults that use similar techniques to ensnare followers and keep them from leaving. I know people who tried to leave an over-bearing religion or cult, and the organization waged nasty campaigns to keep them in the fold. Such individuals had to dig deep into themselves to find the courage to leave, in spite of massive pressure from their family and community. Then they had to hold fast to their choice as they built a new life, even while the family or institution continued to harass and shame them. Such brave individuals grew in ways that far outshined how they would have grown had they stayed in the organization. In a sense, they "hired" the religion, cult, or family to challenge them and help them advance spiritually. From a broader perspective, *A Course in Miracles* tells us that the term "challenge" is inappropriate for a child of God—which we all are—since our true self is greater than any apparent opposition from the outer world.

Geographical and Political Soul Contracts

People who live in a particular city, region, or nation are attracted to be there because they share similar soul lessons. Like individual people, every area has a personality that presents unique gifts and challenges. People who live in the same region often hold similar beliefs and lifestyles, not because the region causes them, but because those people are a match to the values that area represents. Residents could choose to live elsewhere, but they prefer to stay where they are. Someone who grew up on a Midwest farm could not imagine herself commuting to a job daily on a Manhattan subway, while a native New Yorker would go stir crazy in a rural area. Everyone is where they are by preference, always related to their soul choices.

Ask yourself, "How does living in _____ enhance my spiritual growth?" and you will have a key to understand why you are there. People who live in a multi-ethnic urban area experience different learning opportunities than those in a small town with a homogenous population and a relatively narrow worldview. Nations that have been through wars dwell in a different mindset than those less touched by conflict. People in impoverished countries see the world through very different eyes than those in more affluent nations. Where you live physically is strongly related to where you live psychologically.

Soul choices also play out politically. Political leaders and events reflect the underlying beliefs of the masses. Even while we cast votes at the booth, we more fundamentally vote with our consciousness. The world is our thoughts pushed out as nations as well as individuals. It is never an accident who steps into the leadership role in a country. A president or prime minister represents the strongest subconscious choice of the nation's citizens, regardless of how that person entered or stays in office. Everything we see "out there" is a match to what is happening in here collectively as well as personally.

During the past two decades, the United States has elected two presidents who lost the majority of the popular vote, but won the electoral vote. While many people complained that this was unfair, and resisted the person elected, all events follow scientific universal laws. You can complain that an apple fell on your head while you were sitting under a tree, but the apple was simply following the law of gravity, which you can also make work in your favor if you understand it. The dynamics of soul choices supersede the methods we have invented to make political choices. Every political leader reflects the consciousness of the city, state, or nation, for better or worse.

Even in monarchies or dictatorships where citizens are not allowed to vote, the leadership indicates the consciousness of the people. Citizens may just accept the fact that they have no power or voice, or believe that their leaders are always corrupt, or the nature of politics is evil. The population may also have holes in their integrity, which the leadership mirrors. A nation with integrity cannot support a leader absent of it; such a situation would be a violation of universal law. Just as the life of an individual is a perfect expression of the person's subconscious dynamics, the welfare of a country reveals underlying intention.

When the consciousness of the masses changes, that shift is reflected in leadership. Until the past few centuries, *all* nations were ruled by monarchs, many egotistical, tyrannical, or insane. Then the people got fed up with oppression and revolted. They "voted" with their revolution. A revolution simply marks a watershed moment in evolution. The fledgling United States dissociated itself from British rule, the French overthrew their king, and the Russians got rid of the czar. Now nearly all countries function by democracy, and there remain but a handful of monarchies or dictatorships. The consciousness of humanity has generally grown beyond the acceptance of oppression, and politics have changed to express the soul growth of the masses. Of course there remain elements of corruption even in free countries, which is also a statement of the group consciousness.

Political situations offer soul lessons at yet an even deeper level. A nation may elect or accept a self-serving or malicious ruler in order to stimulate dynamic change that would not have happened with a milder leader. A malevolent ruler polarizes the country so that everyone must choose whether they will align with the darkness or make a stand for the light. While that process is never easy or comfortable, the soul strength that the citizens and the country gain advances the nation's evolution immeasurably, and extends to the world. The United States had to choose between slavery and freedom, and South Africa had to choose between apartheid and racial equality. Both nations struggled through the growing pains of such transition—the old guard did not let go gracefully—but they did. The result was a monumental step for each country and humanity. Nelson Mandela being elected President of South Africa, and Barack Obama being elected President of the United States were not a result simply of the number of votes cast, but of a radical shift in the consciousness of their constituents.

Breaking Soul Contracts

If you find yourself in a constricting situation such as an abusive relationship, a job you hate, or a restrictive health condition, you might be tempted to believe you need to stay because you have a soul contract that binds you there. While this may be partially true in that you created the situation for the lessons it offers, it is not wholly true because one of the purposes of the situation is for you to learn how to escape from it. Any situation, no matter how hard, painful, or longstanding, can be healed. Never let go of your vision of wellness. For an inspiring vision of how any condition, no matter how severe, can be healed, study the patients treated by spiritual healer Bruno Gröning (www.bruno-groening. org/en/healings/physical-healings). You will find many inspiring cases of people who rose from apparently unhealable conditions and claimed a new life of well-being.

We learn most sharply by contrast. When you throw a rubber ball against the floor, the amount of thrust behind your throw determines how high it will bounce. A strong throw causes the ball to contract severely, which makes it bounce higher. When you enter into a situation that generates a severe spiritual contraction, as you learn to release yourself from it, you "bounce" higher than if the contraction was milder. Mobilizing the wisdom, courage, and self-honoring to leave a toxic relationship, get out of an oppressive job, find physical healing, or dethrone an abusive leader builds spiritual muscles you would not have gained in a lighter scenario. So the purpose of the soul contract was not to stay in the unhappy situation, but to learn to grow out of it.

Worldly contracts represent the tip of the iceberg of the contracts we make at the level of soul. Your ultimate agreement is between yourself and God. Since you are an aspect of God, that agreement is between you and yourself. You agreed to enter into the house of illusion and find your way to truth. Soul contracts, properly executed, help us achieve that goal. We can celebrate our soul contracts with those who support us, as well as our contracts with those who challenge us. Everyone we meet is our learning partner, every interaction an invitation to awaken. Because you are a soul more than a body, soul contracts provide the perfect means to purify your consciousness so you become aware of your true identity, power, and worth. Every experience, masterfully orchestrated at a level deep below the surface of your psyche, is a steppingstone toward the magnificent illumination you were born to claim.

FROM SOULMATES
TO WHOLEMATES

We all yearn to meet that special someone who will partner with us and make our life complete. Countless songs, novels, and movies glorify the heady joys a romantic relationship promises, along with the painful trials we endure in our epic search for the beloved. For some people, the quest for the perfect partner is the driving force of a lifetime.

But is there more to the pursuit of love than finding the right partner? Are there deeper reasons and lessons associated with romance and marriage? How does the quest for relationship fit in with intentions of our soul and our destiny?

Intimate relationships offer the most powerful opportunities for soul growth. While the journey appears to be about finding someone who will make us happy, we are really learning how to choose happiness no matter our relationship status. We think our soulmate is a person, but it is really our soul. To the extent that a partner helps call forth your soul, the relationship is worthwhile. If the relationship stifles your soul, it is toxic and you must find a way to reinvent the relationship or leave. The former is always preferable, but sometimes the latter is necessary. No matter what route you take, if the relationship gets you more in touch with your true self, the experience has served you well.

Painful Illusions and Healing Truth

While the benefits of joining with a partner are paramount, an unhealthy connection can yield misery. Because we tend to give our power away to love interests, we allow our inner peace to depend on our partner's behavior—never a wise choice. If someone can make you happy, they can make you unhappy. Then you ride a rollercoaster of exhilaration and heartache. You become a puppet of their moods and whims. The wise alternative is to make yourself happy, and not lean on your partner as the source of your well-being, which dwells within you.

All pain in relationships is a result of believing in illusions. It is said, "the truth hurts," but the truth only heals. What hurts is the deception of a mind hijacked by fear. When we recognize illusions for what they are, and reveal the truth they were hiding, we escape from sorrow, and establish ourselves in the fulfillment we deserve. Here are the top five illusions that generate suffering in relationships, and the truths that offset them:

False Belief 1: You are empty or broken, and you need someone to make you whole.

No one can complete you because you are already whole. The more you try to become complete, the emptier you feel. Any action based on a lie reinforces the lie. The false premise in relationships is that you are in need and there is someone who can fill that need. The personality has needs, but not the soul. Relationships work only when we come *from* wholeness rather than seeking it.

Every relationship is an invitation to let your soul shine. When you know the beauty and power you embody, everyone who looks upon you is uplifted and wants to be in your presence. Whole people attract whole people. People who believe they are empty attract people who believe they are empty. Behold the formula for dysfunctional relationships. Two people who think they are lacking come together to fill in each other's gaps, which never works because *you have no gaps*. All *perceived* gaps are the result of an erroneous self-image. Instead of finding someone to prove you are lovable, upgrade your self-image.

Don't expect someone to do for you what only you can do for yourself. When you appreciate who you are, you will attract someone who reflects your self-love, not your self-criticism. You can't blame a partner who criticizes you when you are already criticizing yourself. That person is simply mirroring your unhealed thoughts, so you can shine light on them and heal them. Forgive your perceived flaws, accept the splendor you embody, and you will attract a partner who sees your beauty, not your frailty. Quit identifying with your dysfunction and let your divinity become your identity. You can upgrade an existing relationship by rising in love with yourself rather than waiting for a partner to change their behavior, or attempting to manipulate them. The knowledge of your inner riches is the key to a golden partnership. While relationships appear to be a quest to import your good and validate your worth, they are more fundamentally a journey of self-discovery.

False Belief 2: You have but one true soulmate.

When you set out to find "the one," be careful which "one" you are looking for. You may be searching for your twin flame or your split-apart, but there is only one flame, the light of love that animates the entire universe. You cannot have a split-apart because you have never been split. The idea of a gap is the mother of all illusions. You are not separate from love because you are made of love. Romance promises that when you find the one, your life will be meaningful. If you don't find the one, your life will be a disaster. If you find the one and lose him or her, you are doubly cursed. All such notions are fairy tales spun of fear and lack, and must be dismissed if you are going to know true love.

Your search for the one is justified because the entire spiritual journey is about moving from the two to the one. But the one is not a person. The one is the One. There is one God who expresses through you and all living things. Bodies are many, but Spirit is one. Translate your quest for the beloved to the quest for the Beloved, and you are well on your way to fulfillment.

There are many people who could be a worthy partner for you. What you are looking for is not a person, but an energy; not a form, but an experience. Never define yourself as needy, or define the pool of people who can partner with you as limited. God can and will send you any number of potential right partners. When you quit narrowing the field to one scarce or remote candidate (who often embodies a tragic flaw or disappointing unavailability), you will find lasting love through any of an abundance of great mates.

The ego maintains its grip over us through a belief in lack. Spirit, on the other hand, knows infinite supply. God does not limit our access to love. We do that. When we think with God, we have access to all the partners we could ever want or need.

False Belief 3: You must change or fix your partner so he or she will become who you want them to be.

Falling in love with a partner's potential is not the same as accepting them for who they are. If you can be happy with a person just as they are, you are good to go. If you have a hidden agenda to mold them into the perfect partner, you are setting both of you up for a rocky road that will lead your partnership over a cliff.

It's important to hold a vision of your partner's highest self, but that partner has to be lovable and worthy now, rather than waiting until you have corrected their lower self. You want someone to love and accept you as you are, so why would you love someone only if they change? You bring forth your partner's best self by seeing them that way now, not doting on their defects. When you celebrate who your partner is, rather than who you hope they will become, you free yourself and your partner to find true love right where you stand, not at the end of a fantasy remodel.

False Belief 4: You regard relationship as a destination rather than a journey.

Finding a partner or getting married is but a milestone on a far greater adventure. Wedding rings are circular, symbolizing that there is no ending point to relationship. Union does not start with marriage or end with divorce. Real relationship is a state of being, not an event. Many people get hung up on the form of the relationship rather than its essence. The altar where you speak your vows hosts but a momentary symbol of your connection. The real altar is your entire relationship, which goes on far longer and runs far deeper than a single ceremony or the relationship box you tick on Facebook. If you equate a marriage ceremony with victory or a wedding with relationship, your vision is severely shortsighted. Real intimacy is your ongoing, ever-deepening union with your beloved, using your time together to polish your souls so they shine. True love transcends single moments or specific events. It is an experience that can be captured only in the heart, not a camera; only in eternity, never in time.

False Belief 5: You equate a breakup or divorce with failure.

"Why did your marriage fail?" is a trick question because it assumes that ending equals failure. Just because something ends does not mean it failed. *How* you end is more important than *that* you end. It is possible to part with love, kindness, and respect. If you do, you have mastered your relationship, no matter how long, winding, or rocky was the road that brought you to this point. Parting with anger, guilt, or resentment is far more of a failure than going your separate ways. Yet a bitter parting is not really a failure because the relationship is not over. If there is still emotional energy between you, you will remain in relationship, no matter what paths you choose, until you come to peace in your heart. Some couples use their parting as a way to join. Odd as it may sound, they get closer through their divorce than they did through their marriage. It is not what the bodies are doing that defines a relationship, but what the souls are doing. If you are right with your soul and your partner's, your relationship is a success, whether you live under the same roof or on the other side of the world. There is no distance in the soul's world. When hearts join, separation dissolves. This is how a breakup becomes a breakthrough.

Many Kinds of Soulmates

Romantic partners are just one kind of soulmate. Anyone who calls forth your soul is your soulmate. These are family members who accept you as you are, friends who stick with you through tough times, people who forgive you when you haven't forgiven yourself, a mentor who impels you to your peak performance, and a business partner who co-creates success with you. If a relationship reminds you that you are a divine spirit greater than a body, that person is your soulmate.

Sometimes the quest for a romantic soulmate eclipses another kind of soulmate standing right in front of you. You might be so hell-bent on finding "the one" that you miss the many "ones" who bless your life already. You might overlook the gifts offered by a parent, friend, co-worker, teacher, or counselor. Your current partner with whom you are dissatisfied may be your soulmate in disguise. It's very common for people in relationships to be seduced by the idea that there must be someone better. In some cases, this may be true. In most cases, however, the love you seek is already here. You are forever swimming in an ocean of love. The poet Kabir said, "I laugh when I hear that the fish in water is thirsty." The love of your life is not a person, although a person may be a channel of that love. The love of your life is the fulfillment you experience whenever you let love in or give it out.

It would be a shame to overlook the blessings already given because you are busy looking elsewhere. It's easy to get lost in romantic fantasies; the search for a soulmate can become an addiction. In some indigenous cultures, falling in love is considered a disease and is treated by a doctor as a malady. Western culture glorifies falling in love rather than rising in love. There is much more to true love than romance. Even while you are searching for a partner, your soulmate (which is not a person but a state of mind) might be reaching out to you through people you have written off as irrelevant. No one is irrelevant. Just as every character in a movie advances the plot, so everyone in your life contributes to your enlightenment. Appreciate what you have before asking for more.

Someone who challenges you is also your soulmate. Your personality may be praying to meet someone tall, dark, and handsome, while your soul is praying for someone who will help you gain spiritual strength. Even while a spouse or family member may irritate you, they are helping heal you. Intimate relationships sandpaper our rough edges and polish the diamond we are. In overcoming adversity we build spiritual strength that serves us for a lifetime.

Ultimately, everyone is your soulmate. The purpose of every relationship is for both people to connect with each other's souls. Until you make that connection, you will feel frustrated by thin conversations and hollow encounters. Daily billions of people walk through the imitation of life rather than real life. Only a small number are committed to living at depth. If you are reading this, you are among those who value real gold. When mining material gold, the more you unearth, the less there remains. When you mine spiritual gold, the more you find, the more there is to find. When you are committed to unearthing the soul in all your encounters, there will be no end to the love you experience.

The Mystical Marriage

The search for an external soulmate mirrors your yearning for the union of elements within your psyche. We must learn to integrate the masculine and feminine parts of our self; the rational and emotional; the objective and intuitive; the active and passive; the penetrating and the receptive; the human and the divine. St. John of the Cross urged, "Take God for your beloved." The ecstatic poet Rumi rejoiced in the moments he encountered his Beloved, who was not a person, but God playing peekaboo through many different forms. The desire for a human beloved is a representation of the desire to consummate our relationship with God. The "urge to merge" is a far more compelling instinct than finding Mr. or Ms. Right. We are really searching for Mr. or Ms. Right Here. Scanning profiles on Match.com symbolizes perusing the different parts of our psyche until we find our true self.

I used to have dreams of meeting my soulmate, moments of absolute fulfillment and intense joy. The odd thing about these dreams was that my beloved would show up in different forms. One night I would meet one person, and on another night it would be a different person carrying the same energy. Sometimes the beloved would be my current partner, and at other times someone else. Because each different form carried the same essence, I realized it was not a person I was searching for, but an energy. The movie *Every Day* portrays a 16-year-old girl who meets her soulmate each new day in a different body. One day her soulmate is a white boy, on another day a black boy, and on another day a woman. The next day her partner is her age, and the next day much older. Same being, different package. She is in love with a soul, not a body. This cinematic depiction is closer to truth than fiction. We are in love with a spirit, not the vessel through which the spirit is channeled.

Even while our ideal partner appears in people who show up outside of us, ultimately that spirit lives within us. It *is* us. The universe will never let your fulfillment depend on someone or something outside you. When you become your own beloved, you will be liberated from seeking another person to make you enough. You are either enough, or you are not. There are not degrees of enoughness. There are only degrees of separation. Once your mind made the initial separation from your divine self, an entire universe of separation rolled out in your perception. You will not heal the separation by manipulating the outer world. Only when you restore unity with yourself will the outer world come together. Established in wholeness, you will never feel separate from anyone. All healing occurs from the inside out. When you rise in love with yourself, the door is open for you to connect with someone whose love for you reflects your own self-valuing.

Until that day—which can come sooner than you think—the pain of hollow, conflicted, and broken relationships hides in the folds of the many illusions that have been laid over love. We are now calling those illusions into the light so we may realize their emptiness, release them, and reveal the glorious truths they were concealing.

An Appalling Higher Purpose

Jewish theologian Martin Buber stated, "All journeys have secret destinations of which the traveler is unaware." The quest for a soulmate is the great transformational journey with a hidden reward. In seeking a partner, you may envision snagging a good-looking mate; gaining financial security; obtaining the approval of parents, religion, or society; offsetting loneliness; flaunting a jaw-dropping wedding; living in a prestigious house where you host parties that make the neighbors jealous; and producing 2.3 high-achieving children who bring home soccer trophies.

While all of these goals have value to the human personality, your soul has a far richer intention for relationship. The material and social prizes are the cheese that gets the mouse in the trap that becomes a classroom to grow the soul. The real purpose of a romantic relationship is to reveal the golden nature of both partners that romantic fantasies hide. *A Course in Miracles* tells us that when you discover the true purpose of your relationship, you will be appalled. Coming together has nothing to do with the false reasons you ascribed. To learn to love truly is the only reason for being together. When you see each other as God sees you, you have crossed the only goal line that matters.

Your soul will never be satisfied with the illusion of love. While the ego thrives on fantasy, the soul is fed only by reality. Most people chase love everywhere but where it lives. The answer always seems to be somewhere out there, in the next person or acquisition. Meanwhile your soul rests serene in the sanctuary of your heart, patiently guiding you until you find your way home. Even while you have been distracted by the appearance of love, your soul has retained its awareness of real love. You will surely find your true love, and it will surely be you.

MATCHES MADE
IN HEAVEN

We usually think of a "match made in heaven" as a couple brought together by divine design for a romantic relationship. But the principle of right matching applies to many more situations in which two people or entities join for a seamless fit. Finding the friend, job, home, car, teacher, or any agent or object can be a match made in heaven.

Perfect matches are organized by the Law of Attraction and the Law of Balance. The Law of Attraction connects people and things of like vibration and intention. The Law of Balance provides that if a coin has a front, it also has a back. For every house for sale, there is someone seeking that exact home. For every job opening, there is a person with the right credentials to fill it. For every book, song, or movie produced, there is an audience who will enjoy and benefit from it. No transaction is random; invisible dynamics bring together people who can help each other.

I once purchased an expensive sports car on an impulse. After owning it for a while, I didn't like it so much. I wasn't using it a lot, and the monthly payments were high. I posted an ad on Craigslist, and a fellow showed up who liked the car. But his offer fell short and we couldn't make a deal. We parted cordially and I kept the car. No one else was interested, and I wondered what to do with the vehicle.

A few months later I was having dinner with Ram Dass in a small vegan restaurant in a tiny town, and the prospective buyer walked in with his family. We recognized each other and he asked if I had sold the car yet. I told him I hadn't, and he upped his offer. We did a little more negotiating and we came to an agreement. I sold the car to the man it belonged to.

The next week my gardener asked what had happened to the car, no longer in the garage. I told her I had sold the car to this particular fellow. "Oh, I do his gardening every week after I come to your house," she said. Confirmation of a perfect match.

At another time Dee and I were looking to purchase a house, and we found one we really liked. Upon inquiry, the real estate agent told us that the house had just gone into escrow with another buyer. We were disappointed, but we trusted and figured that if the house was for us, it would end up in our hands. If not, there was a better place for us. A week later the agent phoned and told us that the sale had fallen through, and the house was on the market again. We made an offer, which was accepted, and we moved into a wonderful home we enjoyed for a good number of years. Energetically, the house had our name on it.

If you are worried about finding the right mate, house, job, employee, buyer, doctor, attorney, or architect, take heart. There is a fit for your need. The universe has clever, astounding, even miraculous means to help you connect with the perfect person or thing that will help you both. Affirm:

I know and trust there is a right and perfect match for what I need or I am offering. At this moment that person or object is making its way to me. In spirit, the transaction is already done. In form, we will meet at the perfect time, organized by grace, and I will sell what I am offering or find what I am looking for with ease and satisfaction to everyone involved.

Then relax and trust. The wheels of universal matching are in motion, and the transaction will come to fruition by a divine design in perfect timing. Do what you can to further the transaction, without fear or struggle. Then leave the consummation of the interaction in the hands of Great Spirit. There are invisible forces that bring the right people together for the right purpose.

What is Mine Shall Know my Face

You own what you own by right of consciousness. If you are equivalent in thought, feeling, and intention, the object of your need or desire is yours. It will come to you and stay with you. People have invented all kinds of rules and papers that supposedly prove what belongs to you. Some objects that society says belong to you, do, and some don't. Just because you have a marriage certificate or ring does not mean you are married in spirit. Many people who have a paper or ring do not belong together because they are not an energetic match. Other people have never gotten married in a church or city hall, but their deep love and devotion joins them with undissolvable spiritual glue. Traditional marriage ceremonies cite, "What God has joined, let no man put asunder." More precisely, "What God has joined, no man or woman *can* put asunder."

People have all kinds of warped, archaic beliefs about who should be married to each other and who should not. It wasn't very long ago that interracial marriages were frowned upon, and even now many parents insist that their child marry within the religion. Until a few hundred years ago, all marriages were arranged for social status and political purposes only. In some countries and cultures, they still are. In the big picture, souls are not subject to politics. They follow aliveness and soul-motivated intention. Religious, racial, national, cultural, ethnic, or age differences are irrelevant to the soul. The soul's radar detects only love, kindness, caring, connection, respect, and vitality. All else is detail.

What truly belongs to you comes naturally, easily, and organically. You don't need to force an object you desire to come in the way and time you demand. If you are flowing with the stream of life, everything you need will show up gracefully when you need it. American naturalist John Burroughs penned a touching poem that captures this important dynamic:

Waiting

Serene, I fold my hands and wait
Nor care for wind, nor tide, nor sea;
I rave no more against time or fate,
For lo! my own shall come to me.

I stay my haste, I make delays;
For what avails this eager pace?
I stand amid the eternal ways,
And what is mine shall know my face.

Asleep, awake, by day or night,
The friends I seek are seeking me;
No wind can drive my bark astray,
Nor change the tide of destiny.

What matter if I stand alone?
I wait with joy the coming years;

My heart shall reap where it has sown,
And garner up its fruit of tears.

The waters know their own, and draw
The brook that springs in yonder height;
So flows the good with equal law
Unto the soul of pure delight.

The stars come nightly to the sky,
The tidal wave comes to the sea;
Nor time, nor space, nor deep, nor high
Can keep my own away from me.

Struggle to Get, Struggle to Keep

A sense of struggle is a sign that you have stepped out of the divine flow. The practical metaphysician Florence Scovel Shinn taught, "Struggle to get, struggle to keep." If you have to fight for something, it is probably not yours. Fighting to get anything is an indication that you have drifted from contentment of your soul, your strongest ally to attract your good to you. Struggling to hold onto a mate, for example, is antithetical to what mating is all about. True mates recognize each other and are joined by choice. You shouldn't have to battle with your partner to capture him or her, and then to get that person to stay. You are not required to fend off interlopers. Your partner is not a cache of gold you have to build a fort around and shoot whoever encroaches. If you have slipped into such a mentality, you have fallen way off the mark. Fear-based manipulation has nothing to do with love.

Occasionally you may have to make a stand for what is yours, such as if your partner is tempted to stray, you are in a dispute over child custody, or you are enforcing a real estate boundary. In such a case, fear, anger, possessiveness, manipulation, or attack will work against you. If you can calmly know your right to have a healthy relationship, your kids, or your legal boundary, and establish yourself in the right of consciousness, you will be far more empowered than if you are upset.

In business, work with people who are a match to you. Just because you believe you need something from someone, does not justify a stressful or out-of-integrity relationship. One of my clients was trying to decide whether to accept a deal offered to him by a small company. "I just don't like these guys," he told me. "I feel creepy when I'm with them." I told him that was a good enough reason to turn down the offer. I assured him that there are plenty of people out there who could support his business without him feeling creepy working with them.

Rethink any religious or spiritual path that calls for struggle and sacrifice. Many of us have been trained that if we are not suffering, we are not doing it right. The contrary is true. If you are struggling, you are not doing it right. This is not to say that marriages, business deals, and spiritual paths do not require effort, dedication, discipline, and perseverance. But you can engage in all of those noble pursuits without a sense of angst or fighting against yourself, another person, or a group. Standing for what you believe in is more powerful than battling a perceived enemy. When you drop into a consciousness of warfare, you weaken yourself. ("If God is with me, what could be against me?") When you trust the Law of Attraction, the Law of Balance, and the Right of Consciousness to sort things out in everyone's favor, they will.

Rejection is Protection

If you make a sincere effort to connect with a partner, product, or house, or complete a business transaction, and you are turned away, don't try to force a result. You don't need to pursue what doesn't pursue you. It is said, "Human rejection is God's protection." There is a reason you didn't get it. Something better awaits. Usually you will discover the wisdom and grace behind an apparently failed transaction. I have attempted to initiate many relationships, real estate purchases, and business deals that didn't work out for odd reasons. Sometimes a promising opportunity fell through at the last minute. These are never accidents. A higher hand guided the result. I have learned to never question, argue, or fight over such a fall-through. I trust that if the object was right for me, it would have happened. If not, I am better off. Something better always comes along to replace it. *A Course in Miracles* tells us, "Trust would settle every problem now."

Matches Made in Hell

If you are suffering in a relationship, job, or living situation, you have a powerful soul lesson before you. You may be being shown that your motivation for entering that situation was faulty. Or perhaps you are facing your fear that you will be lost or bereft without this person or job, and you are being called to realize that the abundant universe will take care of you one way or another. If you feel guilty about leaving, you may need to rise above the guilt and leave with confidence. Or perhaps you are being called to heal your negative beliefs that are making the situation so distasteful, and to forgive the other person and/or yourself, master the situation, and stay triumphantly.

Don't crimp yourself into the position of being the victim of a person or situation. There is huge spiritual opportunity here. You may stay or you may leave, but the expansion of self-knowledge is the hidden gift of the experience. Staying or leaving is not as important as *why* you are staying or leaving, and *how*. One of my clients was wrestling with whether or not to stay with his partner. I explained to him that the educational process he was going through in order to come to a decision was more meaningful than the decision itself. He could stay or leave in fear, or he could stay or leave with love. The "why" of things is more important than the "what" of things.

There is a spiritual "why" to every interaction. What comes to you and what doesn't come is guided by a higher hand. The God Who wants you to have everything that matches your good, will send that good your way. If you are busy fighting for something that doesn't match you, it is harder for the universe to deliver what does match you. If you try to rush what matches you, you will miss the blessing of what is before you, and possibly delay your right match coming. If you push away what matches you, it will persist until you accept the gift it is offering. The universe is established in rock-solid, unbendable, hard-wired laws always working in your favor. Your role is to appreciate and respect those laws, and let them help you. All right matches are made in heaven. You can relax, flow, and let life love you by giving you what your heart desires and deserves. The universal matching service is always working on your behalf.

FINDING YOUR
JUST RIGHT TRIBE

In the movie *What a Girl Wants,* a free-spirited teenage American girl goes to live with her stuffy English father. She tries to adopt proper British protocol, but becomes only more frustrated and depressed. Finally her boyfriend asks her, "Why are you trying to fit in when you were born to stand out?"

We might do well to ask ourselves the same question. Do you not fit in with the mainstream, or feel that you are weird, or something is wrong with you? Does your family pressure you to be more normal? Do you have visions, values, and experiences that you worry that others would criticize if they knew about them? Does part of you hide in a closet and hesitate to express your true self, for fear of being misunderstood and rejected?

If so, I have good news for you: There is nothing wrong with you. You are perfectly on track with your destiny. You have just not met your "just right tribe." But you will. Or maybe you have. The universe has ingenious ways to bring together people who belong to the same soul family.

Your just right tribe can be a life partner, certain family members, a small group of friends, like-minded coworkers, a company with values that match yours, or fellow students on your spiritual path. You do not walk alone. You were not born to be isolated and marginalized. There are others—many others—who think as you do, and will gladly welcome you as their own.

Being normal is highly overrated. Being authentic is far more meaningful. In a world where phoniness and disconnection are the norm, why would you want to be normal? A large number of people living in the middle of nowhere does not make it somewhere. Being well-adjusted is not a worthy goal or a compliment. Well-adjusted to what?

If you are a misfit, there is a place where you fit. Being unhappy as a misfit is an essential step to place you where you fit. If you were complacent as a misfit, you would never seek to move to where you belong. Discontent is the initial motivation to becoming content. Let restlessness propel you to your right place. Your experience of "not it" amplifies your intention to find "it," and you surely will.

Your True Soul Family

Perhaps you were born out of wedlock, or adopted, or a foster child, or your father left home when you were young, or your parents divorced. While you might judge your history of a non-traditional or broken family as a deficit, it may be an asset at the level of soul. Even while problematic situations hovered around you, you were on track with your destiny. There are many ways that children find their way to their right parents or family. Biological birth is just one of them. Like normalcy, biology is highly overrated. The journey of the soul has little to do with biology, and everything to do with energy; it is less about the body, and more about the spirit.

Being born out of wedlock means nothing at the soul level. "Wedlock" does not sound like a happy word, does it? It rings something like "padlock," "gridlock," and "lockdown." People being locked together implies bondage. People who choose to be together do not need to be locked together. A friend of mine said, "Marriage is a great institution if you don't mind living in an institution." How about substituting "heartconnected" for "wedlock?" God does not see the rules and requirements that fearful people fabricate. God sees only the activity of soul. Even if you were born of two parents without a heart connection, or you never knew your father, your heart is connected to a much greater support system than your parents. There are many other people willing to give you the love you missed. There are no accidents in the universe, and you are certainly not an exception. You are here for a mighty purpose, no matter how you got here.

I know many people who were adopted, or whose biological father left when the child was young. Or perhaps one parent passed away or divorced and the child lives with a parent who remarried. In many cases, the new parent supports the child immensely and the two bond deeply. In such instances the transition to the new parent was a God job. You ended up with the person your soul signed up to be with. People who truly love each other find a way to be together.

Perhaps you had an unhappy life as a child, no matter how you got to your parents. Someone in your family abused you emotionally, physically, or sexually. While you had a rough start, as you matured you learned to value genuine love, acceptance, and respect. The painful childhood experience motivated you to be a compassionate, caring person. You understand pain and you want to help relieve others of suffering. This entire process led you to find your way to your soul family, or you will. In his brilliant book *Illusions*, Richard Bach declared, "The bond that links your true family is not one of blood, but of respect and joy in each other's life. Rarely do members of one family grow up under the same roof."

I mentioned that world change agents Jeff Bezos, Steve Jobs, and Larry Ellison were adopted. So were Babe Ruth, Eleanor Roosevelt, Nelson Mandela, Leo Tolstoy, Jamie Foxx, John Lennon, and Abraham Lincoln. Motivational master Dr. Wayne Dyer spent the first ten years of his life in orphanages and foster homes. If you were adopted, you are in good company. These people all grew up to find their just right tribe and create staggeringly productive lives. Dr. Dyer used to say, "It's never too late to have a happy childhood."

Steve Jobs, Bill Gates, and Mark Zuckerberg did not finish college. Neither did Michael Dell, Oprah Winfrey, Microsoft co-founder Paul Allen, Whole Foods founder John Mackey, and DropBox founder Arash Ferdowsi. All of these people became wildly successful when they veered from the course they were expected to take, and got on track with the course guided by their soul. Your soul is also guiding you. Never mistake worldly requirements for the calling of the soul. If you are good with your soul, you are good to go.

Click Here

In a world in which many people feel alienated and lonely, masses are hungrier than ever for a sense of family and community. While social media tallies more and more virtual friends and followers, many people have fewer real friends. Posting photos of lunch does not constitute intimate communication. Clicking "in a relationship" does not mean you are truly connected with your partner. The person with the most "likes" is not the happiest or most successful. Souls grow tired of meaningless chatter, counting fans, and hustling to prop up an image. Souls are nourished only when hearts touch.

Like a salmon swimming upstream to return to its home, your soul will keep seeking, searching, and forging forward until you find people you truly click with. Trying to fit with a group you don't click with is like trying to stuff a jigsaw puzzle piece into a space where it doesn't belong. The edges get frayed, you get frustrated, and when you step back to look at the picture, it isn't right. When you give up trying to force a mismatch, you find the right piece that slides in easily and matches the big picture. If you have already found your just right tribe, you understand the importance of being with souls who match yours. If you are still en route, take heart. There are people out there who belong with you and are waiting for you. Don't get discouraged or give up. The universe would not put a desire for soul connection in your heart if the universe were not able to help you find it. The Bible asks, "Would God bring to the point of birth and then not deliver?" God doesn't tease or taunt. If God puts yearning in your heart, that same God will give you the guidance and means to fulfill it.

In the *Star Trek* television episode *Amok Time*, Mr. Spock became possessed to return to his home planet of Vulcan to participate in his culture's ancient mating ritual. That compelling impulse overrode his default logical process. The story models our own journey: When you have a spiritual connection, your soul will commandeer your life to fulfill your intention. Your intuition will keep prodding you to get together with certain people, though you may not know why. Connecting with them is more important than continuing your historical relationships, living up to family or cultural expectations, or following logic alone. While biological mating is a powerful motivator, the desire to belong to a community that matches your soul runs even deeper. Trust your guidance. It will take you to your just right tribe.

A Bigger Island than You Think

I coached a fellow who had just discovered his spiritual path. He was eager to connect with like-minded people, but he complained, "I live on an island and there are no people around me who are interested in a spiritual lifestyle."

"What island do you live on?" I asked him.

"Los Angeles," he answered. "I was speaking metaphorically."

I had to laugh. "There are probably more people interested in spirituality in Los Angeles than just about any other place in the country," I told him. "You just haven't met them yet."

This fellow was surrounded by just right tribe members, but he didn't see them because he didn't believe they were there. What you don't expect is invisible to you until you expand your vision to observe and accept it. My client's metaphor of living on an island was apt. We all live on the island of our beliefs; we are aware of everything that matches our beliefs, and blind to what doesn't. In many cases we don't need to move to another island, but rather broaden our vision of the island we already stand on. Many different realities interpenetrate each other. What you are looking for may be much closer than you know.

Clarify Your Signal

To find your just right tribe, clarify and amplify the signal you are broadcasting that represents your true self.

When you confidently state, "This is who I am," the Law of Attraction will join you with like minds and souls. If you are hiding out, it's harder for people who match you to recognize you. Quit apologizing for who you are, and start celebrating it.

If you are gay, or drawn to an alternative lifestyle, or excited about an unusual career path, or you don't care to watch the news, or your best friends are twelve cats, or you are striving to be a billionaire, or you are drawn to minimalism, or you prefer bold clothes, or you intensely yearn for a life partner, or you would prefer to fly solo, then be honest about where your joy lives. When you stand behind what you believe in, what you believe in will stand behind you. Then, with the least effort or struggle on your part, you will draw to you others who match you.

While your professed goal may be to teach underprivileged children, become a stand-up comedian, or move to Tuscany, you are immersed in a deeper seminar. The spiritual lessons accompanying your physical step are even more important than the three-dimensional step. Your lesson may be about trusting your guidance, expressing yourself unapologetically, breaking from tradition, setting healthy boundaries, or some other variation on the theme of authenticity and integrity. Because you are a spiritual being by nature, all the material elements and choices you make are in the service of your spiritual growth and soul reward. There is a sweet spot where your most cherished material journey aligns with your spiritual path. When you touch that place, everything makes sense.

The Relief of Coming Home

When you connect with your just right tribe, you experience the immense relief of coming home after a long, frustrating journey in a foreign land. Denial of being yourself is burdensome and exhausting, for you are refuting who God created you to be. A Zen master said, "You have no idea of the weight you have been carrying until you let it go." Everything in nature succeeds only by being what it is. Human beings are the only creatures in the known universe who resist our own nature. Dropping that fight and aligning with your true self is one of the most monumental turning points in a human life.

There are people out there who will love, accept, appreciate, and support you for being who you are. Genuine friends do not ask you to change. No one was meant to walk alone, and no one has to. Success is not measured by the volume of people who agree with you, but by the quality of the people who do. A few good friends on your chosen path are more valuable than associating with lots of people who feel like strangers. Kindred souls recognize each other. When you connect with someone in your just right tribe, you know it and so do they. Coming home will relieve you of the awful burden of having to prove yourself or stuff yourself into the mold designed by people who have no idea who you are. You will feel unspeakable relief and excitement about pursuing your unique path. Then you will realize that every step in your journey has been in the service of your reunion with yourself.

WRONG REASONS, RIGHT RESULTS

Have you made a huge mistake that has messed up your life or someone else's? Have you gotten out on the wrong foot in a relationship or job, and wish you could start over again? Do you feel stupid or guilty for missing out on a major opportunity? If you could go back in time and change one decision, what would that be?

If you feel burdened by remorse or self-criticism, or you are on a course you wish you hadn't chosen, take heart. Some of the most regrettable mistakes end up as stunning triumphs. You cannot judge an apparently faulty event because you have not seen the end result. Vision based on judgment is always nearsighted. The soul, by contrast, trusts that all events, including flubs, gaffs, and seemingly fatal blunders, are leading to something better.

Leo Tolstoy had a large gambling debt to pay, so he penned a book to earn the money. That book was *War and Peace,* one of the great literary works of all time. Fast forward 125 years: Bob Friedman, then-President of Hampton Roads Publishing, received a manuscript from a fellow who had been homeless and started talking to God. Bob found the book unworthy of publication and tossed the document in the wastebasket. Bob's daughter, who worked in the office, picked the papers out of the trash, read them, and urged her father to print the book. He agreed, and the *Conversations with God* series by Neale Donald Walsch became an international bestseller.

Four decades before Walsch, a minister wrote a book about how our thoughts affect our life. He sent the manuscript to several publishers, who rejected it. The writer became frustrated and tossed the manuscript in the trash. His wife had more faith in the book, so she pulled it out and encouraged her husband to try one more time. He did, and this time the book was accepted and published. That writer was Norman Vincent Peale, and the book was *The Power of Positive Thinking,* which became one of the most popular motivational classics in publishing history.

Mark Twain, eager to minimize his public life and retreat at home with his family, purchased a huge Connecticut mansion that ran him into deep debt. His obligation was so onerous that he had to reluctantly go back on the lecture circuit to pay his bills. While this motivation seemed to Twain like a setback, many thousands of people received the benefit of his penetrating wit, a legacy that has been passed down through generations. The house and debts came and went; his wisdom ripples through the ages.

The mind steeped in planning is quick to decide what should happen, when, and how. Yet Spirit holds a far broader picture of what will serve humanity, and often brings great things to life through unanticipated means.

Your destiny is not subject to the tyranny of fear-based judgments. It is hurtling forward like a freight train at mighty speeds on track to its destination. Events that you believed were huge mistakes often lead to positive, life-changing results. It is precisely the events that dislodge you from your old path, sometimes abruptly or painfully, that set you on a new and higher course. Thank God for interruptions. They save us from a banal existence. We have been told, "The end justifies the means." More precisely, the end *arranges* the means.

Ideas Whose Time has Come

God dispatches illumination and healing to humanity through chosen books, movies, art forms, and inventions. An open-minded writer, producer, artist, entertainer, or inventor picks up on a potent idea, brings it to life, and enjoys immense success while advancing society. Victor Hugo declared, "Nothing is more powerful than an idea whose time has come."

I once received a manuscript from an unknown writer requesting a testimonial for a spiritual fiction book she was about to self-publish. I gave the book a quick read, and I was not impressed. There were no new ideas in it, the story line was thin, and it wasn't well written. I didn't get beyond chapter two. Wanting to support the writer, I gave her a testimonial that was positive but not raving.

A few months later I heard people talking about the book, which grew into a huge groundswell. To my amazement, the book became a number one international bestseller. Everyone was reading the book and discussing it. I remember stepping onto an airplane and seeing men in business suits reading what I had considered a bland new age attempt. I scratched my head, wondering why this book was so popular, while other books I found far superior were not. I came to the conclusion that the book was simply an idea whose time had come. The universe wanted to deliver a message to the world, and this writer was aligned with that message, and carried the ball. I was, of course, happy for the writer, a lovely person. Some successful forays are a mystery to the reasoning mind.

Sometimes people of poor character get hold of a project that becomes a sensation. They happened to be in the right place at the right time with the right idea, and a huge windfall comes their way. Millions of people get helped, and the world is a better place for their creation. If the person's character is faulty, they have to deal with the results of their integrity gap. When you have a lot of worldly power, your lessons are amplified. If a windfall recipient mismanages money, succumbs to the temptations of fame, or deals unfairly with clients or colleagues, they will learn important spiritual lessons. Everyone has their own learning curve, fulfilling their destiny by way of their unique path.

The messenger is not the message. While it's inspiring when the messenger lives the message, that is not always the case. No messenger is perfect. If you get distracted by the messenger, you may miss the message. If God chooses an apparently inferior person to deliver a superior message, that's God's business. We can judge the person's shortcomings, or we can focus on the gifts they deliver. The person we see is a function of the perception we are using to see them. Ego sees ego. Spirit sees spirit. If you have space for a flawed person to do great things and succeed, you give yourself the same permission. On a human level, we are all flawed. On a divine level, we are all perfect. When we identify with our divinity more than our humanity, we give Higher Power a wide avenue to work through us.

Multiple Channels

Very often several different people or companies latch onto an idea whose time has come. One person or company brings the product to the masses, and gets credit for it. But with a tiny shift of fate, another person or group might have become the legend.

While Alexander Graham Bell was developing the first telephone, Elisha Gray was immersed in the same effort. Bell's attorney arrived at the U.S. Patent Office to file his telephone patent on the morning of February 14, 1876. Gray's attorney arrived at the office to file a similar patent on the same day, hours later. For a century and a half we have acknowledged Bell as the inventor of the telephone. With a slight alteration of events, we might be thanking Gray.

While the Wright Brothers were conducting their experimental airplane flights at Kitty Hawk, a group of French engineers was working on a similar project. But the Wright Brothers got their idea off the ground first, so they got the credit.

You and I were taught that Guglielmo Marconi invented the radio, but the real innovator was Nikola Tesla. Years later, Tesla challenged Marconi for the right to the radio's patent, and the U.S. Supreme Court awarded it to Tesla.

Some people get into legal battles over who is the actual originator of a book, song, business project, or invention. One person or company charges that the other "stole my idea." While in some cases this may be so, more often the product was an idea whose time had come, and several or many people were simultaneously developing it. The fact that the idea came to the world is more important than who brought it. Certainly artists and inventors deserve credit and reward for the gifts they bring to the world. Yet in the biggest picture, the real credit for the idea belongs to Great

Spirit. People don't invent ideas. They channel them. Very often there are multiple channels. The group mind of many people focusing on an invention contributes to the one person or company that gets the credit. Yet those who do not get credit need not despair. There are more ideas where the first one came from.

Pulling Power

A new invention or cultural advance is elicited by masses of people needing, ready, and calling for innovation. Abraham-Hicks calls this dynamic "pulling power." A strong intention draws from the universe the means to manifest it. We understand this principle through the adage, "Necessity is the mother of invention." Deep willingness accelerates the manifestation of the object of desire. The channel through which the object shows up is acting as an agent of the desire.

I learned about pulling power when I was trimming a mature hedge of hibiscus flowers in my yard. I pruned the branches back severely, and it was not long before lots of leaves and flowers returned, more than I had trimmed. The hedge's strong, deep roots connected to extensive branches, channeling water and nutrients from the soil, robustly stimulated more leaves and blossoms to come forth. A smaller plant with fewer roots and wispier branches would not have so much pulling power. The roots of the hibiscus hedge may be likened to the subconscious need, desire, and intention of the masses calling forth the flowers of personal, cultural, and planetary evolution.

Politics are an expression of pulling power. We cannot blame our leaders for the ills and wars that plague the nations of the world, or designate those officials as the cause of societal advances. At nearly every election many people vote for leaders who continue wars and spend vast amounts of wealth on the military. The current annual military budget of the United States is just under one trillion dollars per year. If Americans really wanted to decrease that budget, we could. But the mass pulling power toward military expenditure is greater than the pulling power for taking better care of people and the planet.

Other countries are more interested in harmony than conflict, so that is what they manifested. Costa Rica, for example, disbanded its standing army 72 years ago. To date, that nation has not been invaded, conquered, or abused. It has rechanneled its military budget toward education, health care, and social benefits, with very gratifying results. A recent World Happiness Index ranked Costa Rica #1 in Latin American and #12 in the world. That visionary step to abandon the military was not the result of a few high-minded leaders. The politician who instituted it were expressing the desire of masses of Costa Ricans for wiser use of their resources. In that country, well-being is the primary pulling power, and its citizens are reaping the rewards of that decision. President Dwight D. Eisenhower summed up this dynamic: "People want peace so much that one of these days governments had better get out of their way and let them have it."

The Devil Knows not for Whom He Works

Some great ideas come to life through apparently dark or evil means. You and I may have judgments about how good things should be born into the world, but all such opinions are short-sighted. Spirit sees a far broader picture.

The Internet in its early stages was envisioned as a military tool. Strategists wanted to develop a system by which, in the event of a nuclear war, communication could be decentralized so if a command center was disabled, there would be other points of command to take its place. So while the technology was initially an instrument of war, it has now been co-opted for many benevolent purposes that make our lives better.

At one time streaming video on the Internet was extremely rudimentary, not feasible at all. Images came in freeze frames, and you had to wait for the next frame to load. Then purveyors of sex websites realized they could make lots of money by streaming sex videos, and they hired code writers to speed up the transmissions. That was one of the strongest motivations for playing movies on the web. Now streaming video is used for far more illuminating and socially empowering communications. During the coronavirus pandemic, for example, Zoom and other interactive video platforms allowed billions of people who were physically isolated in their homes, to connect virtually with family, friends, business associates, and educational and medical resources.

The story is told about a man who came to the rabbi of a small village and complained, "Temple members David, Moshe, and Chaim have been up all night gambling." The rabbi smiled and replied, "That's good!" The protester was dumbfounded. "But rabbi, gambling is against the rules of our religion. Aren't you going to chastise them?" The rabbi smiled again. "It's not so good that they are gambling. But later on, when their minds turn to God, they will know how to stay up all night to serve sacred purposes."

All things are neutral. Their value is determined by how we use them. The small self sees not far beyond its nose. The greater self—the true self—recognizes that all objects, events, and experiences serve a greater destiny.

Happy Accidents

Many famous and highly practical inventions came to the world by seeming accident. Just after World War II, Navy radio electrician Percy Spencer was walking near some radar equipment when he reached into his pocket to retrieve a candy bar. To his surprise, he found a melted mess. He guessed that the heat-producing magnetron waves from the radar unit might be the cause. Spencer returned with some popcorn kernels, which popped amidst the radiation. Then he showed a skeptical coworker a raw egg, which blew up in the man's face. Spencer took his discovery into the laboratory and figured out how to harness radiation to cook food. Thus was born the microwave oven.

When Swiss engineer George de Mestral came home after walking his dogs in the mountains, he discovered a cluster of burrs stuck to his pooches' fur and his pants. Curious about how they attached themselves so steadfastly, he spent ten years studying how the tiny tendrils interlocked with their hosts' surface. After a long series of experiments, de Mestral replicated the mechanism with nylon. Now Velcro has countless uses, including fastening your running shoes, holding a watch on your wrist, and bundling computer wires under your desk.

As Scottish physician Alexander Fleming hurried off to his 1928 vacation, he left a cluster of dirty petri dishes in his laboratory sink, including some smeared with staphylococcus, the source of dangerous staph infections. When he returned weeks later, he found that bacteria had grown on the petri dishes, except in some areas where a mold had developed. Fleming placed the non-infected area under a microscope and realized the mold was a rare form of *Penecillium notatum*, which secreted a substance that kept the bacteria from growing. That moment marked the inception of penicillin, for which Fleming received a Nobel Prize, shared with two other scientists who collaborated with him to develop the first pharmaceutical antibiotic, which has saved countless lives.

The universe is brimming with possibilities to help humanity via people who have their antenna up to recognize opportunities in hidden or unexpected places. Destiny is no respecter of tradition, expectation, human personality, or social judgment. It often emerges via unlikely people walking the oddest of avenues. When humanity is ready for an advance, universal mind will find a way to deliver it. The same divine intelligence that chooses the "what" will arrange the "how." Let us be humble to refrain from judging people and events we do not like or understand. They have their place in the grand mosaic of evolution. What appears foolish, bad, or unnecessary in a single moment may be a key element to help or heal one person or all humanity.

Neither be quick to judge your own errors or apparently misguided intentions as outside the plan for your greater good or your service to others. Some of the apparently worst mistakes lead to the most profound transformation and healing. Right thinking reveals blessings where limited thinking sees sins or curses. A curse is an interpretation of the fearful mind. God is not subject to curses, and because you are created in the image and likeness of a whole and perfect God, neither are you. Every event, encounter, and experience ultimately contributes to soul awakening, the noblest purpose of our human journey.

DESTINY BUBBLES

Violet Jessop was an ocean liner stewardess on the 1912 voyage of the RMS Titanic when the vessel crashed into an iceberg and sank, taking over 1500 people to their death. Ms. Jessop was among a smaller number of survivors. Four years later, she was aboard the HMHS Britannic when the ship hit a mine planted by a German submarine, and sank. Again she survived. Before both of those disasters, in 1911, Jessop was working on the RMS Olympic when it collided with a British warship and was damaged, but did not sink. As a result of escaping these disasters, Jessop earned the title, "Miss Unsinkable."

You are not subject to the destiny that others choose for themselves, no matter how many those people number. You have the power to activate a destiny that matches your soul's intentions, regardless of other souls' intentions. You can establish yourself in a "bubble reality" in which you have an entirely different experience than masses around you. Many people speak of "the economy," for example, as if there is one economy that governs all people. It is not so. Even while many people experience one economic trend, other individuals and groups simultaneously live in alternate economies. There are always people who thrive in a bad economy, and others who tank in a good one. What happens to most people does not happen to some. The destiny you carve is your own, independent of the choices of others.

Dutch cyclist Maarten de Jonge was scheduled to fly on March 8, 2014 aboard Malaysia Airlines Flight 370, but decided to take a flight that departed an hour earlier. Hours later Flight 370 disappeared over the Indian Ocean, the strangest missing airplane mystery in history. On July 17 of the same year, de Jonge had a ticket to fly on Malaysia Airlines Flight 17, but changed to a different flight to save money. Flight 17 was shot down over the Soviet Union.

Statistics reveal that the average number of people who cancel or change their tickets before the departure of airline flights that crash is higher than the average number of people who change their tickets for flights that do not crash. Coincidence? Not at all. Everyone related to those flights had their date with destiny, those who were on the planes and those who were not.

Jerry Epstein worked at the World Trade Center in Manhattan. One morning he decided to take a few extra minutes to get a yogurt on his way to work. That morning was September 11, 2001, when the twin towers were attacked and brought down while Jerry sat at a café a few blocks away. Jerry's side trip saved his life.

Were Violet Jessop, Maarten de Jonge, and Jerry Epstein just lucky? Or were they being guided by a higher design? I believe they had a purpose to keep living. What that purpose is, only they can determine through their life that followed.

The Bible tells us, "The number of your days He shall fulfill." We are each here as long as we signed up to be here. We will not depart a day earlier or a day later. While our soul chooses the length of our life, *we* choose the quality of our life. How long we live is not as important as *how* we live. The greatest achievement of a lifetime, no matter how long, is that we live well.

Ultimately we are all unsinkable. We are immortal, indestructible souls who survive anything that happens to our body. Physical ships may go down, but our essence soars far beyond worldly disasters. We are all saved from tragedy because a part of us cannot be hurt and does not die. If all we are is bodies, we are in deep trouble. But if we are spiritual beings, we transcend the troubles of the world. There is a state of consciousness we can rise to, in which worldly problems cannot touch us. The human journey is an element of the greater divine journey. When we attain a mountaintop view of life, we are free of the strife in the valley.

Destiny Makes Visible What Matches It

Everything in form vibrates at a unique frequency. You can see the words on this page because your eyes are attuned to the same frequency at which your physical book or electronic reader is vibrating. There are many frequencies of light now passing through the room where you are sitting, including infrared, ultraviolet, and gamma, that you cannot see because the physical eye is aware of light within a relatively narrow spectrum. You hear only the sounds to which your ears are attuned; dogs can hear all kinds of sounds the human ear cannot distinguish. Everything you notice is a vibrational match to the apparatus you are using to perceive it. Nikola Tesla said, "If you wish to understand the universe, think of energy, frequency, and vibration."

Your soul is attuned to everything that matches your destiny, and not attuned to everything that doesn't match it. You will notice what belongs to you, and remain unaware of what doesn't belong to you. You see what you need to see, and don't see what you don't need to see. This wiring is imbedded at a very deep level.

Author J.K. Rowling submitted her manuscript for *Harry Potter and the Philosopher's Stone* (titled *Harry Potter and the Sorcerer's Stone* in the United States) to over a dozen publishers who rejected it. An editor told her to keep her day job because "you cannot make a living writing children's books." Finally the chairman of Bloomsbury, a small English publisher, showed the book to his 8-year-old daughter Alice, who read the first chapter and demanded that her father publish the book. The Harry Potter series went on to become the bestselling series of books in the history of popular literature, making J.K. Rowling—a struggling single mother who was so destitute that she was stealing diapers from maternity stores—now richer than the Queen of England. The series has delighted, inspired, and educated billions of children and adults all around the world, and spawned numerous blockbuster films.

Was it an accident that little Alice liked the book and told her father to publish it? Not at all. While the adult editors who rejected the book were not attuned to its depth, Alice was. She had the eyes to see the potential of Harry Potter's adventures. Her father was willing to share her vision. The rest is history.

The Beatles, seeking their first recording contract, were rejected by record producers Columbia, HMV, Pye, Philips, Oriole, and finally Decca. Decca executives stated, "guitar groups are on the way out" and "the Beatles have no future in show business." Instead, Decca signed Brian Poole and the Tremeloes because that group lived closer to the recording studio and their travel expenses would be lower than the Beatles'. Eventually producer Brian Epstein heard the Beatles and convinced EMI subsidiary Parlophone to sign them. The

Beatles went on to become the most successful entertainers in the history of the world.

All of the producers who turned down the Beatles did not recognize their talent. Brian Epstein did. He was a vibrational match to their potential. It takes but one person to recognize greatness and proliferate it. Beatle Paul McCartney said of Epstein, "He had a bigger vision for us than we had for ourselves." Destiny finds its way through the crack of least resistance or, we might say, the door of most openness.

If a potential relationship partner, employer, producer, publisher, landlord, seller, or agent turns you down, it is not necessarily an indication of your lack of talent or worthiness. The person rejecting you may not have the eyes to recognize what you have to offer. You are invisible to that person because he or she is not a match to you. It's no mistake if you do not click with someone who does not want you. They are simply redirecting you to your greater destiny. There is another person, or perhaps many, who see with different eyes and recognize possibilities for you that others do not envision. All the companies who rejected J.K. Rowling and the Beatles demonstrate that "there are none so blind as those who will not see."

Protective Destiny Bubbles

Dr. Tatsuichiro Akizuki was a medical doctor who survived the 1945 atomic bombing of Nagasaki, Japan. He stood less than a mile from the epicenter of the blast. In the aftermath, he went on to treat many victims of the bombing. In his research, Dr. Akizuki noticed that people who had a diet rich in miso, a traditional Japanese soybean-based product, had a higher survival rate and were more prone to overcome the effects of radiation that killed many others. Dr. Akizuki published several books on his findings.

While the relationship between miso and health is interesting, the phenomenon points more fundamentally to the dynamic that it is possible for a subset of the population to be protected from danger or disaster while others are not. We might call this a protective destiny bubble.

In an earlier book I mentioned my visit to a small Russian village that traditionally venerated the Virgin Mary. When a plague raged through the surrounding area and took many lives, none of the residents of this village were touched by it. Whether you attribute this miraculous occurrence to the intercession of an angel or to the villagers' faith, the result is the same: they were protected where others weren't.

Psalm 91 poetically describes the phenomenon of protective destiny bubbles:

> He who dwells in the secret place of the Most High
> will rest in the shadow of the Almighty.
>
> I will say of Yahweh, "He is my refuge and my fortress;
> my God, in whom I trust."
>
> For he will deliver you from the snare of the fowler,
> and from the deadly pestilence.
>
> He will cover you with his feathers. Under his wings
> you will take refuge. His faithfulness is your shield and
> rampart.
>
> You shall not be afraid of the terror by night, nor of
> the arrow that flies by day, nor of the pestilence that
> walks in darkness, nor of the destruction that wastes at
> noonday.

A thousand may fall at your side, and ten thousand at your right hand; but it will not come near you.

You will only look with your eyes, and see the recompense of the wicked.

Because you have made Yahweh your refuge, and the Most High your dwelling place, no evil shall happen to you, neither shall any plague come near your dwelling.

For he will put his angels in charge of you, to guard you in all your ways.

They will bear you up in their hands, so that you won't dash your foot against a stone.

You will tread on the lion and cobra. You will trample the young lion and the serpent underfoot.

Because he has set his love on me, therefore I will deliver him. I will set him on high, because he has known my name.

He will call on me, and I will answer him. I will be with him in trouble I will deliver him, and honor him.

I will satisfy him with long life, and show him my salvation.

When you dwell in the knowledge of the presence of God within you and around you, you are not subject to the snares and sorrows to which you might be vulnerable if you believe you are cut off from love. Because you are established in a higher vibration, you have access to everything that matches that vibration, and elements of a lower vibration cannot touch or harm you. They may not even be aware of you. You are protected for a higher purpose and destiny.

This is the comforting, reassuring message of the psalm, which anyone would do well to read and speak if a sense of danger or fear arises.

Hostile Animals Become Peaceful

Anna Breytenbach is a gifted animal communicator who has demonstrated remarkable success reaching the inner being of animals. Anna was called to an animal sanctuary to work with a rare black leopard rescued from a zoo where he had been abused. The large cat had become so aggressive that the zookeepers named him "Diablo." In his new home, he hid in the dark of his small shelter, refused to step outside, and viciously snarled at anyone who approached him. He even injured the sanctuary director and sent him to the hospital for a week.

Anna spent a few minutes tuning in to the leopard, and sensed that he felt wounded because no one appreciated him, and he didn't like his name. She also intuited that he missed two leopard cubs who were with him at the zoo. When Anna relayed this to the sanctuary director, he was stunned. Diablo had originally been caged with two cubs, information that Anna could not have possibly known. Anna assured the leopard that he was now safe, in good hands, and nothing would be demanded of him. Immediately the big cat relaxed and walked out of his shelter for the first time in the six months he had been at the sanctuary. He became docile and friendly, to the point that the burly sanctuary director broke into tears. He renamed the leopard, "Spirit." Behold the power of a gentle intuitive woman touching the soul of a living creature in pain. (Watch the inspiring interaction on YouTube, "The Incredible Story of How Diablo became Spirit.")

A similar story tells of a village in Italy that was being terrorized by a wolf during the life of St. Francis of Assisi. The gentle mystic entered the village and had a heart-to-heart talk with the wolf, telling him that no one would harm him and he mustn't hurt anyone anymore. From that point on the wolf became friendly and didn't bother any of the villagers.

In both cases, a mass belief in danger yielded frightening results for all the people involved. Yet one person established at a higher frequency transformed the situation and created an alternative destiny that blessed everyone.

But What about Everyone Else?

I heard a theologian argue against claiming a miracle when you are saved from trouble while others are not. "An airplane goes down and you are the only survivor. 'It's a miracle!' you exclaim because you survived. But what about the other three hundred passengers who died? There was no miracle for them."

His question leads us to an important inquiry about miracles, protection, and destiny. There are reasons for human events that the intellect cannot fathom. The thinking mind, based on the reports of the physical senses, is aware of a relatively small slice of the universe. While the intellect can explain many things, there are far more that it cannot explain. For deeper explanations, we must go to a soul level.

Regarding the airplane passengers who did not survive, each of those individuals had their own date with destiny. They chose to live for a particular length of time for a particular purpose. When that purpose was fulfilled, they completed their mission. From a human standpoint, this makes no sense because we all wish we could live forever, and we believe there is more for us to do. In the case of disasters, I feel saddened with the families who lost their beloveds. There is nothing simple or easy for anyone involved in a tragedy. I wish that all of those people had survived. But the soul doesn't think like this. It has reasons the intellect cannot embrace. Faith embraces trust that there is a deeper plan than the thinking mind can comprehend.

We now arrive at the ultimate question we must all face and resolve for ourselves: Are we simply bodies that are born, live for a brief period, and die? Or is there a part of us that transcends the wrapping of our skin and the number of times our heart beats? Did those whose bodies perished in the airplane crash go on as spiritual beings? Did they return to God, carry on with their spiritual existence without a physical body, or perhaps return later with a new one? Is a survivor better off for keeping a body when others have lost theirs? These are not simple questions. They deserve deep inquiry. Our entire journey through life is directed toward resolving these questions for ourselves and coming to peace with their answers.

I do not begrudge anyone their humble gratitude when they have been spared pain or loss. A grateful heart is a blessing in any circumstance. We can all use all the miracles we can find. For those who grieve, I feel with them and I do what I can to comfort them. Our noblest role is to relieve suffering wherever we encounter it. The beginning of that service is to relieve ourselves of our own suffering, which puts us in the optimal position to help others find their way to freedom. If you survived a plane crash, I am grateful with you. For those who did not, I honor their reality as spiritual beings and I pray for their release from any kind of limitation, and for their families who love them.

Many parallel realities, even on the Planet Earth, exist simultaneously. The reality in which you dwell is equivalent to your consciousness. Each of us reaps the rewards or the hardships of the perspective we hold. We establish our own destiny with the beliefs, feelings, attitudes, and words to which we give our attention. A positive mind attracts positive results and a negative mind attracts negative results. A loving heart attracts love and generates peace for the giver and all receivers. In every moment we are planting the seeds to grow our future and empower others to fulfill their highest potential. The Greek philosopher Heraclitus put it thus:

The soul is dyed the color of its thoughts.
Think only on those things that are in line
with your principles and can bear the light of day.
The content of your character is your choice.
Day by day, what you do is who you become.
Your integrity is your destiny—it is the light that
guides your way.

INTUITION:
THE DOORWAY
TO DESTINY

My friend Kelli had a ticket to fly on American Airlines flight 11 from Boston to New York City. She was excited about the trip because she was working in the music industry at the time, and she was going to participate in a program featuring Michael Jackson. But as the time of the flight approached, Kelli had an uneasy feeling about taking it. This gut feeling grew so strong that she cancelled her ticket. The reason became clear when on the morning of September 11, 2001, the day she was scheduled to fly, flight 11 was one of the airplanes overtaken by terrorists and crashed into the twin towers, killing all aboard and many in the buildings.

What source of guidance deep within Kelli knew that taking that flight would be so very dangerous to her well-being? Her process of knowing did not proceed from her intellect; she had no logical reason to do this. But the soul has reasons the mind knows not of.

Kelli is not an exception to the rest of us. We are all gifted with a deep intuitive faculty. We are not often aware of it because we do not much use it. As children, we were far more in touch with our inner guidance. We approached people we liked and avoided those whose energy we found repugnant. We ate foods we liked and spit out those we didn't. Some of us had "imaginary playmates," invisible friends real to us, but not to our parents. We lived in a magical state that we didn't think about, but simply knew.

Then we were educated to dwell on the left side of our brain only. We were taught to sit still in a chair for many hours a day and focus on the details of reading and math. A glut of historical facts were crammed into our brains, which we were trained to memorize and regurgitate for tests. While our schooling prepared us to navigate the physical world, it systematically separated us from our faculty of intuition, which guides us far more effectively than our left brain only.

The good news is that our intuitive faculty has not disappeared. It remains fully intact, available for us to access it. If you are struggling to figure out what is your purpose in life, who you should marry, where you should live, and what company to work for, your angst is not because your answers are not accessible. Your angst is because you are attempting to exclusively use your thinking mind, a helpful but limited tool, to make decisions. Meanwhile a deeper mind has all the answers you need, and is happy to provide them if you are willing to consult it, trust what you hear, and act on its guidance.

Hot Soul or Cold?

Your intuition is fully aware of your highest destiny and how to guide you to it. Everything God knows, you can know. This is the depth of the love and wisdom with which the Creator has entrusted us.

Your intuition guides you by empowering you when you step toward it, and deflating you when you step away from it. You may remember the children's game, "hot and cold." At a party, you stepped out of the room while someone hid a small object that belonged to you. Then you re-entered the room and the people in the room guided you to find your object by calling out, "warm . . . hot . . . burning" as you approached it, and "cold . . . colder . . . freezing" as you moved away from it. By following the "hot" signal and avoiding the "cold," you eventually zeroed in and found your object.

Your soul works in exactly the same way to guide you to your destiny. Instead of "hot," your intuition gives you a feeling of joy, aliveness, and inner peace when you step toward your good. When you veer from it, you feel "cold" through a sense of hollowness, depression, or pain. If you are honest about what you feel when stepping in any direction, you will be guided impeccably.

To receive your soul's guidance, you must be open and available, and listen astutely. If you are distracted with trivial preoccupations; emotionally upset; doubtful of the guidance you are receiving; depending on external advice rather than internal knowing; or you are bent on sticking to your ego's plan rather than your soul's, you will overlook or override the inner voice. Then you will make a mistake or create a mess, and say afterward, "I should have listened to my still small voice."

Yet even your mistakes are part of your training. You can redo or correct most mistakes, and head anew in the direction of your guidance. There is always an alternate route to your destiny. Sometimes your mistakes educate and empower you more profoundly than your successes. The apparent mistake was a crucial element in your education. On a deeper level, it was not a mistake at all.

How to Develop Your Intuition

You can develop your relationship with your intuition so you can hear that sacred inner voice loud and clear. Here are some ways to achieve that:

Relax your body. An easeful body is conducive to communication from higher mind. Do yoga, exercise, get a massage, take a bath, nap, or do anything that washes tension out of your system. It's difficult to receive meaningful messages when you are uptight. Cooperate with guidance by putting your body in a receptive mode.

Quiet your mind. The primary reason you may miss hearing your intuition is that your monkey mind overrides your deeper voice. The intellect produces static that interferes with more subtle signals. When you meditate, pray, listen to music, or focus intently on a desirable goal or object, you quell the static. Hypnosis and affirmations also enable you to bypass circular thinking and dive into the wisdom of your superconscious mind.

Quit doing activities that numb or distract you. When you work in a toxic office; sit for hours in front of a computer; watch daunting newscasts; complain or gossip; or worry constantly, you are engulfing yourself in a dense smokescreen that makes it difficult for the voice of guidance to penetrate. Give your soul a break and remove yourself from environments and activities that pull you away from feeling good or thinking clearly.

Writers and other artists complain about "writer's block" or another creative impediment. There is no such thing; no impenetrable monolith descends out of nowhere and stands between you and your creations. You are not a victim of writer's block. You are participating in writer's or other artist's *distraction*, focusing on thoughts and emotions that separate you from your creative impulses. Rather than complaining that you are being blocked, redirect your attention to any object or source that lifts you. Your creativity will soon return because you have transferred your attention from what is stifling to what is stimulating.

Focus on uplifting ideas. Reading inspirational books, watching enriching videos, or discussing big-picture ideas with friends of like mind keeps you in your right mind. Give your intellect something intelligent and empowering to chew on.

Develop a conversation with your guidance. Communicate directly with your soul by asking it for guidance. Many spiritual masters have conversations with God, as if speaking with a good friend. That friend is equally available to you and will hear you and tell you all you need to know.

Trust the timing and route of guidance. Never demand that your guidance come right now or in a particular way. The timing and method of guidance is as wise and impeccable as the guidance itself. Launch your request and then release it. You may get an idea in a flash at an unexpected moment, have a dream, read a sentence that strikes you, or have a conversation with someone who casually says a phrase that speaks to you. Let wisdom find you in the perfect way and timing.

Use a permission slip. You might consult an oracle like the *I Ching*, angel cards, or see a psychic or intuitive counselor. If you are confused or upset, an external consultant may be able to see things you are missing. An oracle card can stimulate you to tap into your inner knowing. Just be sure that whatever ideas you receive resonate with your own guidance. Try all advice on for size. If what you see or hear sits well with you, act on it. If not, let it go. Just because a card or a psychic tells you something, does not mean it is true. You already know what's true. The permission slip is simply an alternate route to connect with your innate wisdom. You can also access guidance directly without a card or counselor. But if the permission slip helps you, use it to your benefit.

Act on your hunches. Your intuition needs you to follow it before it can reward you. Acting on your hunches builds a muscle that gets stronger and more available as you use it. Putting guidance into action is the key to reaping its rewards.

Shared Guidance

If you are seeking guidance in collaboration with a relationship partner or another person or group involved in a project, you can ask for shared guidance. Because your interests are joined, there is usually a solution that will work for everyone, which all members can tap into.

In the many years I have been with Dee, we have had countless decisions to make that affect our relationship, family, home, and business. While at first some of these decisions seemed daunting, or it appeared that there was no solution that would work for everyone, when we have tuned in and asked for guidance, we have come to the same answer. Sometimes we have different opinions, our egos get involved, and we disagree over what would be the best path to take. But when we step back, get quiet, pray, listen, open, and declare our intention, "Please show us what would be in everyone's best interest," we come to a satisfying solution. There is always a win-win if we are open to recognize it.

People intimately involved with each other often share a destiny, or at least their destinies overlap. Spirit simultaneously guides everyone to a common good. Even if destiny calls you to move in different directions, the process will be healthy, benevolent, and rewarding. It is not the form of our lives that matters, but the spirit in which we move through the forms. When two or more people declare their intention for the common good, that intention manifests positive results for everyone.

Intuition as a Way of Life

Some people live their entire life guided by intuition. Many successful people rely on their gut to make important decisions. Amazon founder Jeff Bezos stated, "All of my best personal and professional decisions have been made with heart, intuition, taste, and gut—not analysis." It was not Bezos's intellect alone that has made him so successful. It was his willingness to follow his heart.

I coach many people who feel stuck trying to make a decision. They go round and round, back and forth, struggling to decide which person to date, which car to buy, or which job to take. Such people get balled up because they are trying to think their way through their decision. After a point, trying to reason things out only makes you more confused.

I direct such bewildered clients, "Close your eyes, take a few deep breaths, and place your hand on your heart. Get quiet and ask your deeper inner knowing what it would like you to do." Then I see the client's forehead relax, their shoulders drop, and a smile spreads over their face. Sometimes tears come. They have contacted their authentic wisdom. They have cut through their mental gymnastics and heard the voice of their soul. They recognize what they knew all along, but could not hear because they were trying to figure out their answer with their head. They were living from their neck up. When they drop into their heart, the clouds part and their path becomes clear.

At first, acting on inner knowing feels like a leap of faith. Yet when you have tested that voice consistently, it proves itself and you can trust it. Following intuition then feels not like second nature, but first nature. You are regaining an innate skill. After a while, your guidance becomes so trustworthy that acting on it does not feel like a leap of faith, but an ongoing demonstration that when you trust yourself, everything works in your favor.

Confirm Intuition with Reason

Don't be afraid to hold your intuitive decisions up to the light of reason. Sometimes your passion will be so strong that reason cannot stop it; indeed many great decisions seem unreasonable. In other cases, reason will confirm your inner knowing. In other situations, reason will stop you from making a poor decision.

Several years ago I was approached by a company that produces infomercials (television shows that educate and then sell a product). Their agent told me that this company had been observing my work over a period of time, and they thought that I would be an excellent candidate to do a series of infomercials. Their financial proposal was that we split the cost of producing the pilot—$160,000—and we would share the profits equally. I had access to a credit line that could provide my portion of the investment, so I could have done the deal if I wanted to. I remembered that Tony Robbins became rich and famous through infomercials; he is now a mega-millionaire and perhaps the best-known motivational speaker in the world. The agent then showed me a spreadsheet of projections of potential income for me if the series took off. My share could go into the millions. Visions of big wealth and fame danced through my mind. I was quite stimulated.

Meanwhile a still small voice within me was not convinced. It said, "Be careful. This deal may not be all the company is promising." The agent offered to give me access to three references, previous clients who had done infomercials with the company. This felt like a wise course to pursue, to balance my excitement and the carrot the company was dangling before me, with reasonable inquiry.

The results of my conversations with the references were eye-opening. Two of the people I consulted had lost money on the project, and one had just broken even. The financial projections the company had shown me were unrealistic. I figured that if two losing projects and one break-even was the best the company could do to show me their success track record, there was no way I would make a big investment. I politely pulled the plug on the deal, relieved that I had saved $80,000 of debt and probably a bunch of angst. When I told one of my business associates about the project, she laughed. "I don't really think of you as an infomercial kind of guy, Alan." She was right. I don't even watch television. The project was not a match to me. While my ego was titillated, holding my decision up to the light of reason clarified my path. While your intellect is not your sole source of guidance, it can serve as a valuable asset.

The universe has not left you all alone to figure everything out with a mind that is limited and often distracted by fear and illusions. You have a pipeline to perfect wisdom, like a deep-sea diver has an air tube connected to a boat above the ocean surface that supplies oxygen in an alien environment. We are all swimming in a sea of distortions, the waters choppy and murky with false beliefs and mass insanity. We need a guide that can pierce through appearances and reveal the truth. God has given us the gift of direct guidance. The Creator will lead us wisely at every turn if we are willing to ask for help. Your mind will guide you part of the way home, but your heart will take you all the way.

LOOKING BACK ON
THE FUTURE

*G*ood *Witch* is a delightful movie and television series about a holistic healer who transforms the lives of everyone she touches by offering them compassion, grace, and the benefit of her deep inner knowing. The ultimate life coach, Cassie Nightingale takes negative situations and reframes them to bring solace to troubled people. If you would like some uplifting family entertainment, this series is a great find.

After watching all the *Good Witch* movies and TV seasons, Dee and I decided to go back and watch the series again from the beginning. This time I knew everything that was going to happen down a long and winding road. When Cassie met her love interest, I knew the two would marry and how their marriage would turn out. I knew how the political intrigue in her town would unfold. When a new character was introduced, I knew whether that person would be a friend or a troublemaker. I enjoyed the show from an expanded vantage point.

In the same way, psychics can know the future because to them it has already happened. They are simply describing a movie already produced. This makes no sense to the intellectual mind, limited to data reported by the physical senses in linear time. But linear time is no barrier to the higher self, which is not subject to time. The soul's vision soars far beyond the intellect's vision.

Everything that has happened, is happening, or will happen, is already known in the mind of God. When you tap into this cosmic library, known as the Akashic Record, you gain entrée to all the data stored there. While we all have access to that information, some people are more attuned to it, and they know what will happen before the physical senses confirm it. We call them psychics, clairvoyants, prophets, and seers. But they are no different than the rest of us who share the same capacity. Many people just don't believe in the faculty or use it, so it has atrophied, and the world becomes a very small place because we look upon but the tiniest slice of reality. But those who see beyond the physical senses see more clearly, and recognize a life that gloriously transcends the known universe.

You can know what any psychic knows. God has not reserved wisdom for a select few. Brilliance is the birthright of every soul. "Ask and you shall receive" does not apply only to material objects. If you ask for wisdom, you will receive all you need to know.

Another Way of Knowing

I do not consider myself a psychic, but I am intuitive and I often receive guidance from my inner teacher. Occasionally I get specific information I could not have known any other way. When I was eighteen years old, I had a dream that my father was going to die in five weeks. The information did not seem frightening; it was more of a neutral fact than an emotional experience. I just wrote if off as an odd dream. Five weeks later, to the day, my father had a heart attack and died.

Years later I was standing in a school parking lot after teaching a yoga class, chatting with a few students. I had just taught a lesson on the yoga philosophy of reincarnation, and one of the students was asking me about it. I gave an example: "Let's say you decided to come into this life with Harold and Sylvia," pulling random names from my head. The woman blanched and replied, "Harold is my father and Sylvia is my sister." There is no way I could have known that information intellectually.

One summer while I was working on an organic farm in upstate New York, I was about to drive a dump truck through a small town. As I approached the village, a voice said to me very clearly, "Slow down. Some children are going to run into the road in front of the truck." The voice was so compelling that I took it seriously and I slowed to just a few miles an hour. Sure enough, two little kids who were playing on the lawn of a house by the roadside, ran into the road. Fortunately, I was moving slowly enough that I was able to stop without injuring them. I was certainly grateful to receive that important guidance.

These experiences have shown me that there are ways to know things, including future events, that the thinking mind cannot comprehend. We all know what God knows because our higher mind *is* the mind of God. Yet most people do not access this wisdom because we have been trained from a very young age to depend on the reports of the physical senses only. Our divine identity has contracted to the limits of the body, so we are aware only of what the body knows—a far, far smaller domain than what the spirit knows.

Your higher self gives you specific information on a need-to-know basis. You will be told exactly what will help you and others—no more and no less. I don't recommend demanding to know winning lottery numbers or which stocks to invest in. If that information will help you, it will be delivered. If not, you only hamper your process by demanding. You would do far better to affirm, *"I am an abundant being living in abundant universe in which the Creator provides all I need and more, in clever and helpful ways."* Then you can relax and trust that you will have all the information and materials you need to live a prosperous and fulfilling life.

Where Destiny and Free Will Meet

If the future is already set, does that mean we don't have free will? And if not, why bother making any decisions? But, in the human experience, you can't *not* make decisions. From the moment you wake up in the morning, you have to decide what clothes to put on, what you will eat for breakfast, and how you will respond to the text waiting on your phone. Your shirt will not jump onto your back, cereal will not pour itself into your bowl, and Siri will not answer your text. Even if choosing is an illusion, you have to participate in it.

Decision making is an element of your destiny and propels you toward it. Make your daily choices to the best of your ability, trusting that your earthly path dovetails gracefully with your divine path. At a deeper level than your choice of dress for the day, you have set a course for your life. The wisest part of you has established your path. No external source or peripheral power controls your destiny. Stars, numbers, or genetics don't determine your life. At best, they reflect the deeper choices you have made and provide you with opportunities to make conscious choices. If you use esoteric or physical sciences as tools to grow spiritually, they serve well. If you let them rule your life, you have missed the point. Mercury in retrograde cannot stop you from living at maximal joy and success. Only you can stop yourself. Do not attribute causative power to effects. The only real causation belongs to your soul.

Destiny and free will are not either/or. They are either/and. Not this or that. This *and* that. Both operate simultaneously. Don't try to figure this out with your intellect, which but gets occasional glimpses of the divine plan. *A Course in Miracles* calls us to be humble before God, but powerful in Him. We simultaneously walk the earth and own real estate in heaven. Spiritual mastery requires that we navigate both dimensions without the two competing.

You are free to cooperate with destiny or not. More specifically, you are free to cooperate now or cooperate later. You can take the express train or the local train. *A Course in Miracles* also tells us, "Free will does not mean that you can establish the curriculum. It means only that you can elect what you want to take at a given time."

Destiny and free will are both real and effective within the realm that each one occupies. Make the best choices that you can, and trust that destiny will take you to the best place for your soul to thrive.

The View from the Mountaintop

Occasionally you may glimpse a bleed-through of knowing what will happen as if it has already happened. That's because it *has* happened, and for a moment you are looking back at the future. We call this experience *déjà vu*. Such flashes may feel unsettling because for an instant you are lifted out of your apparently fixed identity in time and space, and transported to a higher viewing point. Your soul is already on higher ground, seeing and knowing all things related to your evolution and destiny. For a moment you not only see and know as your soul sees and knows, but you *become* your soul.

In déjà vu, you momentarily leave your small self behind. That's a healthy experience, as it dislodges you from the limits to which you regularly succumb. If you identify with the ego and personality only, you become fatigued, irritable, and possibly ill. Life becomes a drudgery and you grow confused and ornery like an overtired child who doesn't know what he or she wants. Moments of higher vision are healing and renewing. You can't live in illusion for very long before you are gasping for air like a scuba diver who runs out of oxygen. Your soul needs refreshment. Any moment of soul insight is expansive and exhilarating. You can stimulate such insights with various spiritual practices, but they also come by grace. God says, "My child is growing weary. Let me give him or her a broader vision and a reason to carry on." Then you gain a second wind that sustains you until your caravan arrives at the next oasis.

Home All the While

Behind all human destiny is your divine destiny. Whether you end up with a particular marriage partner, home, or career is secondary to the spiritual journey that underlies all human choices and endeavors. Your only destiny that matters is to find your way out of the world of illusion and come home to reality. This evolution is non-negotiable; there is no other place you can end up because there is no other place that bears any substance or reward. How long that journey takes, and how much hardship you have to go through to get there, is up to you. You are free to make all kinds of choices, but you are not free to extinguish your divine nature. Eventually you will tire of the world and all you will want is peace. When all vain journeys have been exhausted, you will stand where you began, in the blazing light of holy oneness. Then you will discover that everything that will happen, has already happened. The journey you thought you were taking is complete. There is nowhere to go because you have never gone anywhere. When illusions evaporate, you will realize you have been home all the while.

SOUL RETRIEVAL

As a child, I used to lie in bed late at night and hear my neighbor Paul come home drunk and get into horrible arguments with his wife. He couldn't hold a job and he was in and out of jail. Paul was actually a nice guy when he was sober. He was kind to me and pitched me baseballs after school. He had a good heart, but his life was messed up. My mother said, "He is a lost soul."

Is it possible to lose your soul? Do you ever feel like a lost soul? If so, is it possible to get your soul back? Or are lost souls consigned to wander desolate deserts forever?

Some shamanic traditions practice "soul retrieval." They perform certain rituals to get a person's soul out of oblivion and back into their body. This process works metaphorically but not literally. You cannot lose your soul because it is the realest part of you. It *is* you. The one thing you cannot lose is yourself. You can lose touch with yourself, but you cannot become something you are not. You cannot retrieve your soul because it has not gone anywhere. It is right here, where it always has been and always will be. If you are going to retrieve something, retrieve the awareness that your soul is here, now, and forever. Minds and personalities get lost. But not souls.

Other spiritual trainings teach "soul recognition." This is a more accurate term for how to get your soul back. You are reconnecting with your soul, regaining your awareness of it. You are shifting your identity from someone wandering the earth, troubled by pain, to a divine being who has retained the attributes of God, no matter what appearances indicate. Your spirit lives far beyond appearances. Your true self is perfect forever.

Countless dramatic tales portray an individual who has sold their soul to the devil. You can give the devil, or fear-based thinking, access to your soul, and maligned intentions can steer your actions. But the devil cannot own your soul because your soul belongs to God. What God created is not vulnerable or negotiable. Even if the devil gets to use your soul for a while, at some point he must give it back. That turning point is not the devil's choice. It is yours. The moment you turn your thoughts and intentions back to Higher Power, It takes over and your soul is restored to its natural divine state.

Some people who have sunken to the deepest, darkest dregs of human deviance have made glorious turnarounds and become eloquent spokespersons for the light. Starr Daily was the hardest of hardened criminals, serving a very long prison term for multiple bank robberies and offences he committed by age 20. In prison he started fights, incited a riot, and was shut away in solitary confinement. In that morbid cell his hands were shackled to a bar above his head for 12 hours a day, and he slept on a cement slab at night. When the guards brought Daily his bread and water, he spat in their faces. Finally he collapsed from malnutrition and had a vision of Jesus Christ standing before him, silently radiating unconditional love. At that moment Daily felt immense evil draining out of him. He became a changed person, studied the Bible, and wrote two inspiring books, *Release* and *Love Can Open Prison Doors*. Behold a soul as lost as a soul can be, transformed in a holy instant by perfect love.

Soulless Living

While some people perpetrate evil acts that make head-lines, there is a far more pervasive and insidious malady that plagues many more people: soulless living. When we lose touch with our soul and regularly act from fear, ego, and misdirected intentions, we become hollow shells. We go through the motions of living and we may even appear to be happy. Yet our presentation is a cardboard prop. We say the right things, plaster the appropriate smile, compliment the boss, and spout popular catch phrases. But there is no one home. We are running on automatic. I heard a radio commentator say, "Everyone is in pain. Some people are just better at pretending that they are not."

Because the universe is utterly compassionate, and God would not have any of His/Her children stray too far from home, the universe will get our attention and redirect us to reclaim our soul. In some cases the reclamation is sub-tle: you might read a book, attend a seminar, or a friend may give you honest feedback and offer help. In other cases, the reclamation is more "in your face." You might experi-ence a health crisis, a divorce, or a financial setback. Life will do whatever it takes to get your attention. Whether your wake-up call is subtle or gross, be grateful that God has not written you off. Your soul is far too precious to be left unat-tended for very long.

The Answer is Closer than You Think

Many people ask me, "How can I get my soul back?" or "How can I find my passionate purpose?"

I ask such people, "If you had a day, weekend, or vaca-tion in which you had no obligations, and you could do anything that brings you joy, what would that be?"

After a moment's thought, they answer, for example, "I would walk on the beach, play my guitar, and watch funny movies."

"Then those are your keys to get your soul back," I tell them. To find the big-picture passion of your life, act on the little joys you have not been allowing yourself. While beach, guitar, and funny movies may seem insignificant, they will connect you with your authentic self. The more you tap into that stream of life force and live from it, the more vitality you will access. Don't try to restore your soul in a dramatic swoop. If the universe gives you such an experience, so be it. Otherwise, small steps in the right direction will create steady, meaningful progress.

Any activity that makes you feel more alive is good for your soul. Any activity that depletes your life force is a vexation to your soul. Do what brings you life. Quit doing what deadens you. Those two sentences form the shortest and best sermon you will ever hear.

"I Forgot How Big!"

There is a touching scene in the movie *Joe Versus the Volcano* that dramatizes the experience of regaining your soul. After receiving a (fake) terminal diagnosis, Joe takes an ocean voyage to the South Seas to sacrifice himself to a hungry volcano god. Along the way, his ship sinks in a storm and he finds himself floating around the vast ocean on a raft fabricated from his suitcases. One night a huge full moon rises, practically filling the sky amidst a million stars splashed across the heavens. In awe, Joe rises, spreads his arms, and tearfully exclaims, *"I forgot how big! . . . Thank you for my life!"*

Like Joe, many of us have forgotten how big life is, and how deeply we are loved. We have disremembered our Source, our identity, and our destiny. But forgetting is not the same as deleting. The memory of our purpose has been held in trust for us, until we are willing to awaken and claim it. That day will surely come for all of us. We can stimulate it to come sooner rather than later when we appreciate and act on the soul moments right before us.

You are the Camera

When I walk on a local hotel beach at sunset, I observe a fascinating phenomenon. As the sun is about to kiss the horizon, nearly all the tourists on the beach whip out their phones to record the event. Just a handful of people sit quietly and meditatively, taking the spectacle into their heart.

The sunset is a soul moment, when the veil between heaven and earth parts for an instant and we enjoy a sense of peace generally absent from our busy, often scattered day. Yet we attempt to capture the event with our camera rather than our soul. We believe, "If I get it on my camera, I have acquired it." But not necessarily. It is possible to record something in your camera without absorbing it in your experience. The sunset photographers are experiencing taking a picture, not savoring the sunset. I imagine that not many of them look at the photo very much after they get home. Their most vital moments are consigned to their camera, not their heart.

Technology was created to enhance our lives, not substitute for it. We have achieved a bizarre transfer of human experience to images on a screen. We mistake symbols for the thing they represent. While hiking in a forest with a friend, we came to a patch of wild peppermint. "Wow, that smells just like my favorite gum!" she commented. Actually, the gum smells like peppermint. No matter how many chemicals the gum-makers use to replicate the aroma, it will never be as pure or soul-stimulating as the real thing. Nature has become inverted in our mind. We would rather stare at a picture of nature than bask in it, chew gum reminiscent of a divine aroma rather than absorb our senses in the real thing.

When we become mesmerized with artifacts that but simulate soul moments, we lose our sensitivity to genuine soul moments. Watching a sailboat race on television is not the same as getting out onto the water. Becoming engrossed in a lovemaking scene in a movie is not the same as making love. Reading about a political candidate who has effected positive social change is not the same as running for office or volunteering at the local youth center. Simulated experiences can stimulate our passion, but that passion has not achieved its potential until we live it.

Even while rampant technology leads us around like a rancher pulling a bull by a nose ring, a part of us yearns to enjoy the simpler, more innocent elements of life. While Steve Jobs was masterminding the digital revolution that completely changed the way we purchase and listen to music, he used to go home at night and listen only to music on vinyl records. He preferred the warm, natural sound of old-fashioned recordings over the cold, impersonal digital sounds he was introducing to the world. The man who was largely responsible for putting the world on screen wanted a respite from it.

The yearning for innocent experience is the heart's way of guiding us back to our source. God wants to feed your soul with real music, magnificent sunsets, delicious lovemaking, and other exquisite experiences. But those gifts are incomplete until you allow yourself to receive them. You are the camera with which God is photographing creation. You are the vinyl record containing the warmest music. Your soul is the repository in which the most meaningful memories are stored. To retrieve your soul, receive the gifts offered to you freely, generously, and forever.

No matter how much your soul has become tweaked, crimped, or hollowed, or how far from it you have wandered, you can reclaim it in a far shorter time and with far less struggle than it took to sever you from it. A plant that has wilted can rebound with watering and daily sustenance. Soul retrieval is not a one-time event in which you dramatically get your soul back and then stay with it forever. Your soul requires daily care and feeding. In the next chapter we will look at how to achieve that. For now, simply know that you can live with an enlivened soul every day if you choose to do so. There is hope for you and for every human being.

You can lose a relationship, job, or house, but your soul is the one thing you cannot afford to lose, or you could really lose. When you are ready to reclaim your soul, the universe will send you all you need to achieve that precious goal. The same God that gave you your soul will give you the means to live from it. No matter how much you have compromised your soul, your soul cannot compromise you. Only in dreams can you lose what you are. When you awaken, you realize that you have retained your golden nature no matter what the dream purported. God has imbued within you Its perfect essence, which cannot be watered down or destroyed. Life can be only life, and because your nature is life, creation lives through you.

SIT DOWN TO
THE BANQUET

The world was touched by the music of gifted singer Karen Carpenter, who uplifted millions of people with her angelic voice, but tragically died at a young age of an eating disorder. Such physical starvation is a manifestation of soul starvation. People who have a hard time accepting food have a hard time accepting love. I know of a woman who healed many women with eating disorders by taking them into her home and constantly affirming their preciousness and lovability.

We all suffer from the eating disorder of undernourishing our spirit. You and I take time each day to feed ourselves in many ways. We eat several meals; stimulate our emotions with music, drama, and poetry; and exercise our intellect by reading, taking courses, and solving logistical problems. But how much time do we spend feeding our soul?

You can survive for a short time without physical food, but without the nutrient of spirit, you will become energetically malnourished over time. If you try to fulfill soul hunger with things in the outer world, you will only grow more frustrated. We have all tried many substitutes for love, yet remain hungry. The answer to psychological pain is not more possessions, relationships, sex, money, drugs, building an empire, mindless distractions, or neurotic self-fixing. It is more soul.

Any investment you make in your soul will yield the most valuable payoff of your life. You may invest in the stock market, real estate, or precious metals. Yet when you take stock in yourself, that market will never crash. The estate of your soul is more real than any earthly property. The essence of your spirit is more precious than any mineral. All worldly investments take a back seat to honoring yourself.

Jesus likened the kingdom of heaven to a banquet. He said, "Come, for all things are now ready." Heaven is not simply a place you go when you die. It is an experience you enjoy while you live. Many gifts have been laid at our doorstep. To receive them, we must cease running to and fro and distracting ourselves with endless searching. What we seek, we already have. What we wish to become, we already are. The turning point of a lifetime comes when we cease to reach outward, and look within.

Soul Starvation Does Not Please God

Some religious or spiritual traditions advise that if you deny what makes you happy, you will please God. They tell you that suffering brings you closer to heaven. But you cannot get to heaven by way of hell. The only purpose of suffering is to guide you to take a different path. Starving your soul is definitely not on the menu of what brings happiness. To the contrary, anything that makes your soul more alive is a key to your destiny. You can hurt yourself by over-indulgence, but you can also hurt yourself by becoming so Spartan that your soul becomes emaciated. After Buddha had experienced extreme opulence and intense self-denial, he realized that neither polarity was the answer to suffering. He advised his disciples to follow the middle path.

Whenever you observe yourself or someone else suffering and you believe that God's will is being enacted, counteract that debilitating belief by telling yourself, "God wants me to be happy. The happier I am, the more pleased God is." May we all turn our minds and hearts to the true will of God, that we may experience the peace that God created us to know.

It's Up to You

You must take the initiative to feed your soul and keep it fed. No caped crusader is going to fly in through your window, turn off your computer, drag you to your favorite restaurant for dinner with your friends, make an appointment for your massage, and send you on a Hawaiian vacation. People who love you may encourage you toward those soul-nurturing activities, but you must choose to do them, or they won't happen. When sustaining your spirit becomes more important than playing out the dictates of fear, habit, and social programming, your soul will thrive.

The moment comes in each of our lives when we must claim responsibility for our happiness. God will help you, but you must do your part. You have many opportunities to be kinder to yourself, doorways to peace you have not walked through. Most people work too much, put unnecessary pressure on themselves, and hesitate to ask for what they really want. They turn down invitations their heart is yearning to accept, and worry about the future. They are generous with others, but not with themselves. Good receivers, on the other hand, ask for what they want and say yes to the gifts that come their way. All is given, but you receive only the portion you are willing to accept.

Decision making is a golden opportunity to practice following joy rather than guilt or fear. When a choice is placed before you, try each option on for size and note which one sits best with your soul. Be honest about where your happiness lives. Then act on the soul-nurturing choice. As you do, you will feel tremendous relief, deepen your relationships, and magnetize success. Life is already lined up in our favor. We just need to line up with life.

Don't Apologize for Being Happy

Some people feel guilty about doing what they love. They believe they are somehow cheating when they should be sacrificing, or their joy takes away from the good of others. But happiness is not a pie with a fixed quantity, and when you grab a slice, other people get less. Happiness is an energy that radiates from your soul and stimulates other souls to join you. You don't need to apologize for being happy. Your well-being is your gift to the world. When you deny yourself delight, you gain nothing for yourself or others. When you shine, you are fulfilling your soul's purpose.

Guilt is not of God; it accomplishes nothing. Guilt issues from the ego, which denies joy where it lives and seeks it where it is not. If you feel guilty about anything, you have stepped away from God's will. God does not judge, see sin, or punish. These are all twisted human perceptions we project onto God. While we believe we need to suffer to pay off sins, God simply loves us and patiently waits for us to come home to love. When your soul is at peace, God is most pleased. To apologize for feeling good is an oxymoron. Why would you say you are sorry for being what you are and doing what God intended you to do?

When Dee and I put our house up for sale, the first thing our realtor did when she entered the building to show it was to turn on all the lights. Buyers are more attracted to purchase a house that is well illuminated than one that is dimly lit. Selling a house is a metaphor for selling any product or service, creating a healthy relationship, or presenting yourself to the world. When your lights are on, people want to be in your presence and support you. Guilt and apology draw shades on the light of your soul. Joy, self-confidence, and expressing your gifts allow your natural radiance to shine. Jesus said, "You are the light of the world. Don't cover your light with a basket." Don't be a basket case. Be a lighthouse.

Regenerate

We all deplete our soul during the course of life on Earth. It is a rare person who is not fatigued by worldly activities. For this reason, we need to restore our soul on a regular basis. You don't just get a vibrant soul at birth, and it stays radiant for a lifetime. You have to participate in keeping it vibrant. A lake needs an inlet and an outlet. If water continually flows out but is not replenished, the lake will run dry. If you are not regenerating, you are degenerating. If you are not composing, you are decomposing. If you are not expressing, you are depressing. Your energetic inflow must equal or exceed the outflow. Soul renewal is not a luxury. It is a necessity.

Feeding your soul is not a mystical, cosmic pursuit. It simply means doing what makes you happy. You might stroll through a forest and listen to the song of the birds, go to a concert by your favorite band, toss your overnight bag in the back seat of your car on a moment's notice and visit your best friend in another state, get a long massage, buy a new outfit, paint with water colors, or join a seminar by an author whose books you love to read. Anything you feel better after doing it is a worthwhile investment of your time and energy.

Here are some more ways to restore your soul:

Deep, sound sleep allows your mind to withdraw from the constant chatter that chips away at inner peace throughout the day. With the monkey mind out of the way, your soul can refresh and renew you. Your body knows exactly how to heal, if you give it a chance.

Meditation, prayer, and spiritual practices align you with the divine presence and allow healing and blessing to fill you, and then stream into the world to help others.

Creative expression like music, dance, art, or writing opens the channel for Higher Power to reveal itself. When you act as a vehicle for great ideas and arts, you are the recipient of the positive energy coursing through you. When you create, the voice of God is speaking through you.

Regular refreshment breaks from your work or routine provide a reset that will give you the energy to carry on through your day. Fifteen minutes of renewal will recharge your battery and make you more effective when you return.

Physical exercise pumps life force through your body and spills to your spirit. Yoga, martial arts, working out, walking, jogging, swimming, and sports get you out of your head and into your experience.

Immersing yourself in nature lifts you to the pure vibration of your original innocence. The natural world functions at a frequency higher than most human affairs and the density of city life. When you walk in the woods, swim in a natural body of water, or lie on the grass and feel the warmth of the sun on your skin, you re-tune to the vibration equivalent to your soul.

Self-pampering with massage, aromatic baths, hot tub, sauna, and spa treatments is not decadent or self-indulgent. The refreshment you gain will relax you, clear your mind, and give you the inspiration and energy to be there for others.

Relaxing hobbies such as reading novels, woodworking, flower arranging, painting, golf, watching uplifting movies, or expressing any passionate personal interest allows your soul to breathe.

Connecting with people you value opens your heart and reminds you that you are loved, important, and not alone. Sharing intimate moments helps you feel safe, validated, and nurtured.

Kindness and service move you out of egocentricity and open your heart. You cannot simultaneously help someone and feel depressed.

While you have likely heard and spoken the 23rd Psalm many times, you may not have realized the soul-refreshing imagery it instills in your subconscious. Being protected by a kind shepherd, lying down in a green pasture, and sitting beside quiet water provide inspiring models of self-care. My favorite verse is "He restores my soul." God wants you to get your life back. When you know that you deserve peace more than pain, peace shall be your predominant experience.

The abundant universe is begging you to accept its gifts. People are willing to support you, material supply has your name on it, and physical health is eager for you to enjoy it. Your blessings are lined up like airplanes approaching a runway, requesting clearance to land. Your ideal scenarios need your cooperation to manifest. If you were as kind to yourself as you are to the people you love, you would rise in love daily. You would glow and those who look upon you would be inspired to keep their flame burning. Unpleasant situations will evaporate as you remove yourself from toxic environments and you release negative thoughts. Dark scenarios will be replaced with loving, empowering experiences. All because you found the courage to say "yes" to your soul.

Karen Carpenter did not die in vain. People in the public eye offer crucial life lessons to those who observe and learn from them. Some teach us what to do, and others teach us what not to do. Perhaps, because of that dear woman's untimely death, more people have become aware of the need to let love in, and lives have been saved that would have been lost. If we dedicate ourselves to feeding our soul rather than starving it, we can avoid suffering that no one deserves. To discover that God's will for you is only happiness, and let your soul shine, is the achievement of a lifetime.

BODY AND SOUL

My friend Ronni was so attractive that she became a successful model at a young age. Her natural blonde hair, blue eyes, and supple figure put her on the fast track in Los Angeles, where she rubbed shoulders with celebrities and men pursued her. She lived in a swank apartment, went to parties at the Playboy mansion, and earned lots of money jetting around the world for glamorous photo shoots. In many ways she was living an ideal life.

Yet despite her enviable lifestyle, Ronni was miserable. She labored under a scant diet that left her constantly hungry, the scale became her enemy, and she freaked out if she found a wrinkle. With fierce competition in her industry, she worried constantly about losing her looks, and she avoided marriage and children because her breasts might sag. She came to mistrust men, most of whom wanted her for her body, and she was jealous of other women whom she perceived as more attractive than her. While Ronni hustled to prop up her image as a happy, healthy woman, she was anything but that. Her stunning exterior housed an empty shell of a soul.

Eventually Ronni had a nervous breakdown and went to live at an ashram where she became a certified yoga instructor. She exchanged her Rodeo Drive wardrobe for loose, natural-fiber clothing, let her breasts live at whatever altitude they chose, and could look in the mirror for the first time without finding half a dozen things wrong with her appearance. "My yoga class brought me peace that nothing in my crazy life was able to deliver," she told me.

When the body becomes the focus of a person's world, it is at the expense of the soul. People who are rewarded for having an attractive body, being an athlete, or working in any industry that depends on youth and beauty, tend to become fixated on appearance and performance. While it's practical to make an attractive presentation, and admirable to cultivate physical health and athletic skill, the temptation to highlight the body can become a major distraction. If you are going to magnify beauty, let it be the beauty of the soul. Actress Sharon Stone, at one time regarded by many as a sex symbol, said, "I don't believe makeup and the right hair-style alone can make a woman beautiful. The most radiant woman in the room is the one full of life and experience."

We all have to figure out how to live in a body on Planet Earth. We must eat, sleep, take shelter, travel from place to place, negotiate space in crowds, thread our way through traffic, channel our sexuality, and deal with pain when it arises. It is a rare person who does not spend a great deal of time focusing on the body and its needs.

Some people make the body their enemy. They call it evil, deny it comfort, and attempt to beat it into submission. They may even glorify physical pain. I know a fellow who joined a monastery where the monks were instructed to beat themselves with small metal hooks until they drew blood. If you saw your child doing that, you would be shocked and recognize that he or she was seriously disturbed. You would do everything in your power to restore your child's well-being. God does not want you to suffer any more than you want your children to suffer. Yet we do things in the name of religion that no sane person would condone. What a strange idea of God we have created! Hurting yourself physically is just another form of turning the body into an idol. To battle the body is to give it just as much power as indulging it—maybe more. What you resist, expands and persists. Struggling to suppress the body is an ego seduction, as the body maintains its grip on your attention at the expense of the soul.

Is there a way you can function in your body so it doesn't stifle your soul? Can you be good-looking, physically fit, and enjoy your material journey without getting trapped? Is there a way to be active in the world and remain established in a higher reality?

There is. Your body is neither good nor bad, god nor devil. Its value depends on what you use it for. Enlightenment does not require you to deny the physical or set it up in competition with the spiritual. Life mastery is a matter of focus, purpose, and priority.

You have seen movies in which the camera focuses on a character in the foreground, while the background is blurry. Then someone enters the room, and the person who entered comes sharply into focus, and the original character becomes blurred. Your soul and body are the two primary characters in the movie of your life. If you focus intently on your body, your soul becomes obscured. If you are absorbed in your soul, your body fades to the background of your awareness. In deep meditation or mystical experience, the body disappears. It didn't really go anywhere; your mind was just occupied elsewhere. The more you focus on the body, the more immersed you become in the world of the body. The more you focus on your soul, the more real your soul becomes. Your attention is the strongest currency at your disposal; whatever you look at grows in your experience.

While riding on an airplane, I was listening to an uplifting spiritual lecture I had downloaded on my phone. Then the in-flight movie came on. I was sitting in the front row of the cabin, where a video monitor sat squarely on the wall in front of me; it was virtually impossible not to watch the film, a vapid teenage romance. As I listened to the lecture with the greater part of my attention, and casually tracked the plot of the film, I learned a profound lesson in how to integrate the physical world and the soul. Be aware of the nonsensical movie, but keep your mind established in the higher lecture. Then you will stay in touch with the silly plot just enough to navigate it, while the greater part of you remains immersed in a more meaningful conversation.

A Telephone to Humanity

A Course in Miracles tells us that the most valuable use of the body is as a communication device for Spirit to express in the world. It's like a telephone through which the divine speaks to humanity. The body is a means, not an end. When the body becomes a goal unto itself, we become distracted from the spiritual gifts the body is intended to deliver. Truth is the message and the body is the messenger. If you are using your body to transmit love, blessing, and healing to the world, you are using the body well.

The purpose of an automobile is to take you from place to place. Yet some people become so enamored with their car that the vehicle becomes the object rather than the method. If you purchase an expensive car, dress it with all kinds of doo-dads, and polish it daily, but you keep it in the garage because you don't want it to get dirty or dented or have someone steal it off the street, the car is not serving its function. Visitors may "ooh" and "aah" over the fancy machine, but it no longer serves the function of transportation; it is a museum piece, an idol at whose altar you worship. You would have a lot more fun with the car if you used it to drive through breathtaking country, go to a workplace where you express your passion and talents, and connect with people you enjoy.

Likewise, your body is designed to take you places, not be a place unto itself. More specifically, it can take you to spiritual places by making the world more like heaven as you use your physical experience to deliver love and healing. Any other use of the body will leave you frustrated and wanting.

The Big Question

Because we have lost touch with our true selves, self-knowledge becomes the driving quest of humanity. When the website ask.com (a search engine predecessor of Google) came out, the most commonly asked question was, "Who am I?" If you do a Google search for that question today, you will get about 9,800,000,000 results. That's almost 10 billion—an awful lot of people asking, "Who am I?"

Because we have hurt ourselves with the great contraction of consciousness, the answer to our suffering is a great expansion of consciousness. We must identify ourselves as spiritual beings more than physical forms. To know yourself as a soul is the great liberation. Souls do not live in fear, get sick, or die. As expressions and extensions of God, souls are healthy, perfect, and immortal. Your body will die, but your soul will not. To confine yourself to a body only is to squeeze yourself into a very small box, moving from a huge mansion into a tiny closet. Can you imagine the owner of a sprawling manor with lush gardens, living in a minuscule dark enclave under a staircase? When you throw open the closet door and step into your divine estate, you reclaim the kingdom you were born to rule.

Souls Transcend Time

Bodies live in time and are bound by it. Souls are not subject to this false and arbitrary limit. Great souls and the ideas they promulgate live forever. The bodies of Jesus, Moses, Buddha, Mohammed, Lao Tse, Confucius, and other spiritual masters walked the Earth thousands of years ago. But their essence lives on like a star whose light continues to radiate throughout the universe long after it has gone nova. Spiritual masters are focalizers of truth, like magnifying glasses that catch rays of sunlight and direct them so intently that they start a fire. Great teachers capture big ideas and use their bodies to transmit them to humanity. Their bodies disappear, but their ideas live on. If you want to live forever, communicate what is eternal.

Motion pictures provide a compelling illustration of the foreverness of the soul. They extend the spiritual presence of the people they depict. Dee and I enjoy watching videos of painter Bob Ross, a gentle spirit who painted amazingly realistic and inspiring landscapes, and taught viewers to do the same. Bob passed away in 1995, but his essence lives on through his videos and paintings, which emanate his child-like essence. We savor his recorded programs as much for his soft demeanor as for his art. Though Bob's body is gone, his soul lives on. Everyone who is touched by his television program and painting is making contact with Bob's soul. He has disappeared in form, but his spirit is very much alive.

Likewise, your departed loved ones are not gone, and neither will you be. Death cannot curtail a soul. You can easily communicate with beloveds who have passed. They are just on the other side of a curtain. The more you connect with them in mind, heart, and spirit, the flimsier and more transparent that curtain becomes. Time and space cannot constrict an immortal being. Love is timeless and deathless. Because your nature is love, you, too, are timeless and deathless.

Take the Gift and Get the Realm

The frequency at which the body functions keys you into everything that matches the body. The frequency at which the soul functions keys you into everything that matches the soul. My teacher Hilda Charlton had a dream in which she was shopping in a bargain store and she bought a cheap pair of shoes. Then the dream turned into a nightmare where she was caught in a world where everything was flimsy and unsubstantial. Buying the cheap shoes trapped her in a cheap world. She titled her lecture, "Take the gift and get the realm."

Every realm brings its own gifts, for better or worse. When you accept the gift, you inherit everything in the equivalent domain. The body is a match to all things three-dimensional. The soul yields access to all things spiritual. Some gifts are pure, and others are Trojan Horses. Shiny objects often disguise traps and pitfalls. Take care which gifts you seek and receive. Each one you accept will lead you to more of the same.

All Kinds of Bodies with or without Soul

Your physical form is just one kind of body. There are many others. Your house is a form of body. So are businesses, religions, and nations. Any entity is a body. The word "corporation" means "body"—like "corporeal" or "corpse." Corporations also have souls—or lack them. Everything I have said about the relationship between a soul and a body applies to larger bodies like companies, cities, and nations. Everything that exists in a form is animated by a soul, or else it would not have any life. No physical body, company, or country can survive without soul force behind it. Soul force created the entity and maintains it. When that soul force is withdrawn or becomes corrupted, the entity dies. All entities are inert; neutral; devoid of their own reality or intelligence. Only the wisdom and power of soul gives life to the form it inhabits.

Your house is a shell that takes on the nature of the people who live in it and the activities that occur there. A house has no will or intelligence of its own. If you love it, maintain it, and place meaningful objects in and around it, the house glows with life and inspires those who enter it. If you are not present in the house, do not love it, and do not care for it, it becomes dilapidated and a physical eyesore or spiritual vexation. You and your family are the soul of your house. If that soul is thriving, the house is truly a home. If that soul is starving, you cannot call it a home. Bodies make houses, but souls make homes.

Your body is not your home; it is a house you temporarily inhabit. If you use your body in a loving way, it is a glorious vacation rental. If you don't use your body to channel love, it is a nuisance and distraction. The saying, "home is where the heart is," is perfectly accurate. We can equally rightfully say, "home is where the soul is."

Two Uses of the Body

The ego has its use for the body, and so does the soul. The ego's use of the body is to make it a god, while the soul's use of the body is for it to serve God. Ego uses the body to stifle the soul by creating endless preoccupations that draw our attention away from love. Spirit uses the body to magnify the soul. You can tell which source is guiding the body by the amount of serenity you experience. Fear, upset, conflict, and pain indicate that ego is in charge. Inner peace is the sign that your life is aligned with your soul.

Because the body is neutral, the purpose you assign to it determines the quality of your life. Worship the body for its own sake, and you are subject to all the dangers and frailties the physical world poses. Use the body as a bridge to connect with others, support and heal them, and you have turned it into a sacred vessel. Your body is the ship that carries you across the ocean of *samsara*, illusion. Keep your sails high and catch the wind of spirit, and you will hasten to your home port. The body is not your enemy and it does not need to be defeated. The body is friend to those who recognize its true potential. Fear is the only enemy, overcome only by love. When fear seizes the body, painful acts ensue. When love guides the body, blessings follow. The harmony of soul and body is the master symphony we came to perform and celebrate. When we achieve this noble goal, we remember why we are here and we fulfill our divine destiny.

My friend Ronni retired from modeling. She got married, had a baby, teaches yoga, and distributes essential oils. She is no longer consumed by her appearance. Although she has put on some weight, bears some stretch marks, and a few streaks of gray highlight her hair, she is more beautiful than ever. She has found a way to let her soul shine.

GENERATIONAL
HEALING

Native Americans say that when you heal a painful element of your life, you heal for seven generations to follow you, and seven generations that preceded you. While it's obvious how you pass your healing down your lineage, how is it possible to heal generations that came before you?

All families tend to transfer their karma to their offspring. Children are prone to manifest the physical and psychological diseases of their parents. If one of your parents was alcoholic or abusive, you may repeat the pattern. If your parents fought a great deal or divorced bitterly, you are likely to have troubled relationships or avoid them altogether. While many parents bless their children with healthy role models, others bequeath a dark legacy.

Newton's first law of motion states that "an object in motion tends to stay in motion unless acted upon by an outside force." When healing from the core, that outside force is really an *inside* force—the soul. If you have a propensity toward some inherited malady, and you tap into the strength of your soul, you gain the capacity to rise above the issue and heal it. When you know that you are more than a body, you are not subject to the laws of the body to which most people give their power. Doctors and psychologists cannot explain many "spontaneous" or "miraculous" healings; such incidents defy the laws of science. (For an inspiring overview of healings that go beyond medical expectations, study the books and videos of Dr. Jeffrey Rediger.) Such phenomena are perfectly scientific in accord with a higher law. *A Course in Miracles* urges us to remember, "I am under no laws but God's." The laws of the soul supersede the laws of medicine and all the limiting laws to which human beings subscribe. When the soul rises to the fore, all worldly bets are off.

If psychology were true to its name, it would honor the reality and power of the soul. The word "psyche" is a Greek word meaning "soul." We tend to equate the psyche with the mind because we believe that our rational mind is who we are and where our answers live. Yet no one can heal at the level of the intellect only. Our true nature and identity run far deeper than the scattered, confused, and generally insane thoughts that dominate our mind and life. Real psychology proceeds from the soul, infinitely more potent than the frenetic mind that perpetuates the dysfunctions that plagued our ancestors.

If you do what your parents did, you will replicate the lives they led. If you live in the same city, eat the same diet, work in the same profession, marry a similar spouse, go to the same doctor, attend the same church, join the same political party, watch the same news, talk the same gossip, and harbor the same judgments and opinions, your life will be a carbon copy of your parents'. If you come from a happy, functional, close-knit family, all of these elements will work in your favor, so you do well to continue.

Yet many people wish to grow beyond the norms and patterns their parents demonstrated. If your parents were in pain physically, emotionally, or financially, and you choose a more conscious path, you will escape their suffering and so will your descendants. You will break the karmic chain. It is the duty of every new generation to release themselves from the tyranny their parents were unable to escape.

A New Person Creates New Results

Many of my coaching clients report, "I went through a bad divorce. Now, years later, I am reluctant to get into another relationship because I am afraid I will repeat the one that didn't work."

I ask those clients, "Are you the same person who married that partner, went through those problems, and divorced that person?"

Every single client adamantly answers, "Certainly not!"

Then I ask, "Have you learned from the experience, changed, and grown?"

They all respond, "Definitely."

"Then you are not likely to repeat your past mistakes," I explain. "As a new and wiser person, you will generate new results."

So it is with generational healing. If you have carved a new course that transcends the patterns that ruled your ancestors' lives, you will not replicate their painful results. You are not a static entity. You are a spirit more than a body, an energy more than a thing, a dynamic being with the propensity to outgrow who you were last week, month, year, or many years ago. Don't limit yourself to who your parents were or who social or scientific opinion tells you that you will become. The person you were is gone, a thought in your mind, an image in your imagination. It has no more reality than a sunny day or rainstorm that came and went last year. Like the mollusk that outgrows a shell, leaves it behind, and spins a new, larger one, a new life awaits you beyond the old one.

Why Hurt People Hurt People

If you dwell on your parents' faults or complain about how they messed you up, you reinforce the errors you yearn to grow beyond. All of our parents made mistakes. They were human beings. The more attention you give the issues, abuses, and traumas your parents fostered, the more you bind yourself to them. At the early stages of healing, it is necessary to acknowledge pain that you have suppressed. But then you must advance beyond it. Don't keep yourself trapped in the box prescribed by those sorrows. There is so much more to you and your parents than appearances purport! Your parents, like everyone, had their souls shrunken to a tiny proportion of their true nature. They were subject to *their* parents' pain. I coach many people who were impacted by an abusive parent. I ask them, "What was your parent's relationship with his or her parent?" In every case, my client reports, for example, "My father's father was as mean to him as my father was to me—even worse." An abusive parent suffered tremendously. He or she did not have the awareness or tools to heal their pain, so they passed it along to you. This does not excuse or condone abuse of any kind. Yet it does give you insight and compassion into why and how hurt people hurt people.

Healing from the Level of Soul

The key to all healing, including generational, is to identify with your soul more than your body. At the level of soul you own the power of the universe because everything God is, you are. You will not end a particular karma by manipulating your personality or attempting to control others. The word "personality" comes from the Greek word *persona*, meaning "mask." Your personality is the mask worn by your soul. It has no causative power. Your personality cannot choose; it is the effect of choices you make at a far deeper level. To heal yourself, the generations that follow you, and the generations that preceded you, you must work at the level of soul.

Twelve-step programs are effective because they acknowledge and call upon a Higher Power. The personality that tries to heal addiction is the same personality that is addicted. You are putting the fox in charge of the henhouse. The personality does not have free will or the leverage to effect transformation. The soul does. When you claim your identity as a spiritual being, you gain dominion over all personality dysfunctions and any challenge that may confront you. Your higher self commands the lower self. This is why prayer is your greatest resource when you are confronted with an apparently unsolvable problem. Prayer is your link to the power of God. There is nothing that God cannot do, including healing an addiction, generating prosperity to sustain you and your loved ones, and resolving the most difficult relationship rifts. If you are going in circles and every day, job, or relationship is a repeat of the last bad one, you are trying to do it all yourself. The efforts of the personality will fail. The efforts of God will succeed. Be humble enough to ask God for help, and worthy enough to receive it.

Healing for Your Ancestors

In Western culture many people believe that when our ancestors die, they are gone. Yet they live on with us and through us. Asian cultures recognize the presence and worth of their ancestors. Many Asian families set up altars with photos of their forebears, and conduct regular prayer ceremonies, sometimes daily, thanking and honoring their ancestors. We in the West would benefit greatly to do the same.

The best way to honor your ancestors is to live the life they wanted for you. All parents want their children to have a better life than they had. Many go to great lengths and endure sacrifices so their children will stand on their shoulders. My parents were children of immigrants who came to America from Europe, essentially penniless. Those immigrants worked hard to make a better life for themselves and their children. Neither of my parents even started high school. They had to go out and work in Brooklyn factories to help support their large families. When they grew up, they took demanding blue-collar jobs. My father was a bus driver and my mother worked at a hat store during the day, and in a factory at night. They sweated so we could move out of the slums and I could go to college. My happiness was more important to them than their own. My happiness *was* their happiness.

By grace, my life has progressed far beyond anything they knew. I live in a nice house in a natural setting, with my loving partner and furry children. In my career I enjoy deeply rewarding connections with my clients and peers. If my parents were to return and see the good they have bestowed upon me, they would be stunned to see how my life has evolved light years beyond theirs. I credit my parents with paving the way for the blessings in my world. Their soul-sourced efforts opened many doors for me. They were uneducated and unsophisticated, but supremely loving, caring, and supportive.

My parents also had their problems. They grappled with some emotional and physical issues. They had judgments and arguments with family members. They smoked a lot. At one time they purchased a new car, but returned it because they could not keep up with payments. They had archaic notions about sex and relationships. They were subject to the flaws, prejudices, and hardships of that generation.

I like to believe that the strides I have attained reflect well on them; that they are looking down from heaven and smiling to know that they launched a life better than the one they knew. Their goal to make me a fulfilled person has succeeded. Through me they broke the chain of karma that bound them through their fears and misconceptions. My life is my thanks to them.

Likewise, your life blesses your ancestors. Who you are is the culmination of what they strove for. You may have your issues and challenges, as we all do, but you have gone beyond what they attained, which validates them for their contribution to your well-being. Even if you have not achieved a higher standard of living, if you have grown spiritually so you embrace a broader vista of life, you have moved your family's leading edge forward. If you appreciate your parents, though they were not perfect, you return the gifts they gave you and you expand on them.

If your parents were unconscious and did hurtful things to each other and you or your siblings, and you have difficulty appreciating them, consider your life a contribution to their healing. If you learned from their example and you would not make the same painful choices for yourself, you are healing that dark cycle. You have joined with them to learn and master hard lessons. They set up their lessons by making mistakes; you finished those lessons by correcting them. It is no accident that you are in your family, no matter how loving or dysfunctional it was or is; everyone in your family agreed to share a particular path that would liberate a segment of humanity from suffering, beginning with your own healing.

If your parents are still alive, you have a golden opportunity to heal while they are here. Don't wait until they are gone to work out your issues with them. You can resolve with them spiritually after they pass, but to do it now, in the flesh, is the most liberating route. Even if you can't change them, or they do not understand, support, or agree with you, you have the power to change your mind about them. That is where the deepest healing lives. Upgrade your vision of your parents so you see them through the eyes of compassion and appreciation. If your heart comes to peace about your relationship with them, you bless them and maximize their ability to choose peace for themselves.

Perhaps you have made mistakes you believe reflect poorly on your family. Maybe you struggle with an addiction; or you have been married more times than most people date; or money is a constant vexation; or you have ongoing battles with family members; or you have legal troubles; or you have secret sins you believe would shame your family if they were known. But despair not. The game is not over; you are still in process. The record books don't show the score at halftime. At some point your current difficulty will be resolved. You will understand why it happened and you will be empowered by the lessons it has bestowed. The strength of character you gain will bless your family now, historically, and unto the generations that follow.

The Triumph of the Soul

Bodies, personalities, and experiences come and go, but souls are forever. You are intrinsically connected to the souls of your ancestors and your descendants. You live not just for yourself, but for and with all of them. Your hardships are theirs, and so is your success. Before acting, ask yourself, "How will this act affect the souls of my family, past, present, and future? You have made and will make mistakes, but you have also made and will make far more strides. Don't beat yourself up for your errors. Celebrate your achievements. It's not your soul that berates you for your errors; that's the voice of ego, finding yet another way to keep you downtrodden in a false sense of inadequacy. Even while your ego chides you, your soul remains perfect, intact, and shining with all the attributes of the God you believe is outside you, but lives within you *as* you. When you remember and identify with your soul, you rise to wholeness and healing that transcends anything that has ever happened in your family, or ever will. Your soul reconciles all human errors and claims victory over fear, loss, sorrow, and death. Now you can say, as psychology trainer Gary de Rodriguez proclaimed, "I stand on the shoulders of my ancestors' tragedies and declare triumph, and know that they are cheering me on."

WHERE YOUR SOUL
GOES AFTER YOU DIE

Early on my spiritual path I attended a Christian worship service. After the service, one of the congregants gave me a little cartoon book that depicted an after-death experience. The cartoon showed a man cowering before a cosmic judge, pleading for mercy for his sinful life. The judge was not moved. "Off to hell with you for eternity," he commanded. The story was obviously designed to scare you into being a good person or following the precepts of the religion. I didn't join that church.

Since that time, I have learned that fear and healing have nothing to do with one another. I have gained far more generous models of a God of mercy rather than one of retribution. I have learned that grace supersedes karma, and the sins we believe will hold us back, are forgiven. Jesus spent a great deal of his ministry freeing people from religious judgments. He was a teacher of release, not bondage.

The soul doesn't go anywhere after death because it has never left somewhere. The body drops away, and we resume our identity as the shining spirit we were before we crammed ourselves into an Earth suit. Unlike the physical body, the soul is invulnerable and eternal. When we apply the limits of the body to the soul, we indulge in stifling anthropomorphism, the projection of human attributes onto God. The soul is not a blob of ectoplasm that floats out of the body and roams the universe like Casper the Friendly Ghost. The soul is an identity of extraordinarily expanded awareness. To recognize the soul, we have to see it through eyes other than the body's. To see the soul, we must use soul vision.

To ask, "Where does your soul go after you die?" is akin to asking, "Where does a literary or cinematic character go when you turn the last page of the book, or watch the final scene of the movie?" The character ceases to be encased between the covers of the book or within the opening and closing credits, and re-emerges as the expansive idea that gave birth to the individual expression. What happened to Don Quixote, Ebenezer Scrooge, George Bailey, and Yoda when their respective books and movies were complete? Nothing happened to them at all. They continue to live in the minds and hearts of those who love and learn from them. To many people, those characters are more alive than the person working in the cubicle beside theirs. We love great literature and cinema because we meet souls with more color and depth than most people who walk the Earth. We need larger-than-life characters to remind us of how good it can get when we set our souls free rather than stuffing them into painful corsets of oppressive social definitions.

Your soul does not live in your body. The soul has a life entirely independent of the body. No matter how finely you dissect a physical organ or how many magnifications under a microscope you study it, you will not find your soul. Your soul exists in a dimension uncapturable by flesh, which is—no offense—just meat. What matters is what moves the meat, and for what purpose. Your soul animates your body, but is not contained by it. While the body sleeps, the soul awakens. When you are free from the endless daily distractions that grab the body's attention like a glittery mobile dangling over a baby's crib, the soul emerges fully present. This is why you have visionary or prophetic dreams. With the physical senses suspended, your soul sense comes to the fore and delivers wisdom and inspiration muddied by the bedazzled physical apparatus.

Your soul is fully intact and alive while your body walks the world and after it returns to dust. The three-dimensional world in which you seem to be an entity separate from your soul is a dream—*Maya,* as Buddhists and Hindus call it. During moments of illumination, you recognize the emptiness of the world. We have all had *"aha!"* experiences when for a flash we poked our head out of the sphere of false containment, and glimpsed a vaster reality. People who have near-death experiences, ingest psychotropic substances, dive deep in meditation, or have a religious epiphany, momentarily step into a reality far more substantial than what appears to be physically solid. When you leave this world, temporarily or permanently, you don't go anywhere. You simply escape the spell of believing that you went somewhere. If you are God, and God is everywhere, then you are everywhere. The soul reemerges as the great *I am* after a short and generally frustrating foray into a twisted fairy tale. The happy ending emerges when we awaken from the dream. You will not sleep forever. Destiny has a grander idea for you.

Death as a Work of Fiction

You cannot die because God is life and all that God is, you are. You can no more separate yourself from life than you could separate heat from a fire, light from the sun, or a wave from the ocean. What is one cannot be divided. The body dies; that is irrefutable. But the real you is immortal. Instead of asking, "Where does your soul go when you die?" we might more appropriately ask, "Who do you become after you lay your body aside?"

The 23rd Psalm asks us to affirm, "Even though I walk through the valley of the shadow of death, I will fear no evil." The operative word here is "shadow." Death seems real because for a moment a false idea has blocked the sun like a passing cloud. But the cloud cannot remove the sun; it can but for a moment obscure it. When the cloud passes, the sun remains. When the illusion of death passes, the reality of life remains.

The most sacred prayer in Judaism is, "Hear O Israel, the Lord our God, the Lord is One." The operative word in that prayer is "One." Jesus reaffirmed this truth: "If your eye be single, your whole body will be filled with light." When we see ourselves clearly, we know ourselves to be the light, not the vessel that carries the light. Light, life, and love are all facets of the same self that cannot be marred or defeated by the slings and arrows of a cruel and confusing world. In God there is no fault or flaw, and because we are one with God, there is no fault or flaw in us, including the ultimate vulnerability, death.

Fear is not of God

While visiting a shrine in Japan, I observed a grandmother strolling the grounds with her five-year-old grandson. When the boy started to wander off the pathway, grandma became frustrated and bellowed, "If you don't stay close to me, the King of Hell will come and take you!" I shuddered to hear this, as the woman was teaching the child to behave under fear, threat, and guilt. I work with many Japanese people who are petrified to do something wrong, lest they be riddled with guilt and shame. I am certain that someone in their family threatened them like the boy's grandma did. It's not just the Japanese who attempt to control through fear, or feel controlled. Many religions and cultures are masters of manipulation. They have figured out that if you can make a person afraid or guilty, you can control them. If religions deleted fear-based rules, there would not be much left of the religion. True religion is founded in love. The Dalai Lama said, "My religion is kindness."

Controlling through threat of a horrid afterlife is very convenient because the afterlife is a mystery to those yet to enter it. It's easy to project morbid stories onto the blank screen of the unknown. Yet more and more people who have experienced momentary death report that on the other side of the veil they found only splendor, release, and unspeakable peace. Most people who have had a near-death experience say they did not want to return to the world. Yet something drew them back because they had unfinished business. After glimpsing heaven, they no longer fear death because they know it does not exist.

Some people who die for a short time report scary purgatorial or hellish experiences. I do not believe these are accurate representations of the world to come. I believe that such people have taken their human fears or beliefs with them, which distort their vision of heaven. If they could rise above what they were taught by punitive clergy or family, I believe they would emerge into the same glorious light that most near-death-experiencers report.

You don't have to wait until you die to go to hell. Many people live a hellish life while walking the world. Hell is not a post-mortem sentence. It is the experience we generate when we think and act outside of love. Scaring people into behaving according to our wishes only magnifies hell on earth, for the controller and the controlled. When you use fear to manipulate others, you reinforce your own fear. There is no hell in love (although we have twisted the idea of love to create hellish relationships that have nothing to do with love). Your defense against damnation is to realize that love exists right where you stand, in you and around you. The opposite of love is not hate; it is fear. When we remove fear from our experience, we instantly and naturally return to love, which is always here, waiting for us to claim and enjoy it.

Why Wait for Heaven?

You have also been told that you have to wait until you die to go to heaven. This is another ploy in the ego's playbook of tricks based on chasms and delays. The ego's favorite mask is "gap." There is always something that has to happen first before you can be at peace. You have to lose twenty pounds, increase your income, build six-pack abs, find your soulmate, have a baby, get your book published, move to Sedona, or build your dream home. When you get to the other side of the gap, you will be in heaven. But, as you have noticed, as soon as you traverse one gap, another gap appears, promising that when you get to the other side, you will *really* be in heaven.

It is entirely possible to know our wholeness and find deep inner peace before we cross any more gaps. We can touch heaven before we lay the body aside. Diving into rewarding spiritual practices, immersing ourselves in activities that bring us joy, and being with people we love connect us with heaven now. One of *A Course in Miracles'* most poignant questions is, "Why wait for heaven?" You don't have to wait until you die to be happy. Do it now and beat the rush later.

There is no afterlife because there is only life. Nothing can come after something that always is. The forms through which life expresses change, but the life that expresses through them is constant. All speculations about an afterlife are distractions from the life here now. Why would you be wondering about an afterlife if you were fully present in this life? While a great deal of attention has been given to near-death experiences, we would benefit more by studying near-life experiences. Rumor has it that there are many people who have come close to living, and they are still here to tell about it. Quit worrying about where your soul goes after you die, and attend to where your soul is going while you live.

A Course in Miracles tells us that in no single instant is death real. You are alive while in a body, there is a momentary shift, and then you are alive without a body. You were here, and you are still here. When the spiritual master Ramana Maharshi lay on his deathbed, his disciples pleaded with him, "Master, don't leave us!" He smiled and answered, "Where could I go?"

Your soul doesn't leave you because you *are* your soul. Only the body leaves. When that happens, you are left with who you were before you became a body, and who you will always be. The introduction to *A Course in Miracles* neatly sums up the truth about you:

> Nothing real can be threatened.
> Nothing unreal exists.
> Herein lies the peace of God.

YOUR ULTIMATE
DESTINY

A round the turn of the twentieth century, a European man named Frederic had a dream to travel to the United States. He gathered all of his savings, booked passage on an ocean liner, and set sail on his adventure across the sea.

Considering that he could not afford the luxury meals the cruise ship offered, Frederic brought with him a supply of cheese and crackers. While the other guests sat on plush chairs in the ornate dining room enjoying opulent multi-course meals, Frederic sat outside on a wooden bench on the deck, rationing out his simple meals for the duration of the cruise.

One day another passenger passed Frederic eating his meager dinner. "Why are you sitting out here eating cheese and crackers?" the fellow asked.

"I can't afford the dining room meals," Frederic answered.

The passenger laughed. "Don't you know that the meals are included in the price of the voyage?"

Frederic, astonished, put aside his cheese and crackers and entered the lavish dining room he deserved all along.

The second half of his voyage proved far more enjoyable than the first.

Like Frederic, many of us settle for compromised rations in life while we are entitled to a lush banquet. We choose goals we believe we can attain rather than those we really want. We set our sights on objects the world tells us are important rather than those that fill our soul. We believe our highest destiny is to find a spouse and have a family, ascend to the top of the corporate ladder, or see our name in lights on Broadway. While all of these destinies have relative meaning, we still hunger for ultimate meaning. Part of us realizes we have a purpose greater than any act we accomplish in the world.

Our highest destiny is to know ourselves as divine beings, whole, perfect, and blessed, heirs to the soul fulfillment bestowed upon us by God. We yearn to return to the great *I Am* from which we came. Our journey through the physical world is fleeting. The Earth is not our home. We are all just visiting this planet. Eventually we will tire of searching for answers where they cannot be found, and find answers within us, where they live. We travel to exotic lands to learn what the world is, but all we discover is what the world is not. The world we have been shown is not heaven; what contains elements of hell cannot be heaven. Yet we can elevate the world to a heavenly experience if we change our mind about it. When we know ourselves as souls more than bodies, our connection with ourselves, each other, and God replaces painful separation. Heaven is not a place we go. It is the discovery of what we are.

In the meantime, we each follow the path before us as a parent, teacher, artist, entrepreneur, caregiver, friend, carpenter, programmer, or any other role to which your soul is guided. Your calling is no accident. There is a place and a role for you in the world. You do not need to leave the world to find enlightenment. Many enlightened beings passionately participate in life. Never discount or deny your heart's desire to express your unique talent, passion, and vision. You are here for a supremely important reason, no less valuable than anyone else's. Many people in humble occupations or incognito lifestyles deliver more healing to the world than others in positions of prominence. It is not *what* you do that matters, but *how* you do it, and *why*.

All of our personal destinies flow into the greater one, like streams that merge into a great river that becomes the ocean. All you need to know is your next step. Many people get hung up trying to figure out their life's purpose, while they overlook what is right before them. Making a query phone call, starting your blog, or asking a certain person for a date may seem menial and uncosmic, but everything is connected to the cosmic. The Great Plan is operating behind the mundane. Your life is important right where you stand.

Be not deceived, dismayed, or distracted by external pressures to perform in ways that do not belong to you. Those who need you to follow their path fail to see that it is *they* who need to follow their path, not you. Insecurity masquerades as proselytizing. Families, religions, cultures, and cults may pressure you to stay in the fold. But you cannot unfold from within the fold. Your soul yearns to be birthed into expression. Let it. The word "permission" is formed of two words: "per" and "mission." "Per" means "according to." When you give yourself permission to fulfill your destiny, you are living per your mission, on track with what you came to do.

Your Incomparable Calling

There is only one person who can live your destiny, and that is you. Be not distracted by comparison or competition, tricks of the small mind. The destiny of other persons is irrelevant to yours, except what you learn from observing how they live their truth or don't. You must do what you came to do, and only you can do it. Have the courage to carve your own pathway, even if no one else has preceded you. When you clear a path through a forest, you open a way for many who will follow. Don't seek or expect acknowledgment, or be dismayed by an apparent lack of results. It is your own thanks, and God's, that rewards you. Many people are like skittish animals afraid to approach or test something new. But if your offering is sincere and connected to Spirit, the right people will recognize you and join you. And if no one else ever does, it doesn't matter. You did what you had to do. That's all that God asks of you. The results are in the hands of the universe. Don't waste time keeping score. The most important scoreboard is invisible to the human eye, but obvious to the soul.

The Great Homecoming

All destinies fuse into the light. You will recognize the insubstantial nature of all things in form, and because you no longer value them, they will disappear. They served as vehicles for your journey home, but when the trek is complete, they are no longer required. Buddha taught that a raft is valuable to take you across a river, but when you arrive, you leave the raft on the river bank. If you try to drag the raft on land, what was an asset becomes a burden. Better to leave the raft for those who come after you, to traverse the waters you have crossed. When temporary destinies have served their purpose, you can let them go. Past steps were meaningful to lead you to where you now stand. One day you will leave all past steps behind and take the great leap into All That Is.

Coming home to God does not mean you will lose your identity. To the contrary, you will leave behind all false identities and claim your true self. Loss seems real only to the ego. In Spirit, loss is impossible because you *have* everything and you *are* everything. When you let go of the unreal, only the real remains. While you seem to be searching for a partner, money, job, or house, you are really searching for love, your internal riches, your divine vocation, and your spiritual home. The things of the world but symbolize the gifts of God. Material objects fall short of fulfilling us because they are but symbols. Your destiny calls you to rise above symbols and claim the experience they represent.

A Course in Miracles promises, "A happy outcome to all things is sure." Yet we can argue, "but that child died," or "that person remained disabled," or "so many species are becoming extinct." In the world of form, many outcomes are not happy. But outcomes in appearances are not the same as outcomes in Spirit. We must lift our eyes beyond the world defined by time, space, and bodies. While life appears trapped in unhappy forms, or the spark of life leaves a body, there is far more to life than forms and bodies contain. They are the vehicles through which life expresses, but they are not the sum of life or its source. We are either spiritual beings or we are not—that is the ultimate decision we must make. If we are physical beings only, we are limited to a suffering world, and our struggles lead but to the grave.

But if we are spiritual beings, the hardships of the world cannot daunt us. We soar high above the battlefield. Jesus said, "In the world you shall have tribulation, but be of good cheer, for I have overcome the world." He and other spiritual masters call us to rise to the consciousness they attained. We achieve that crucial leap not by action, but by grace. We do not need to earn what we already deserve. God's love for us is unconditional and eternal. When we realize that we *are* the love we seek, everything unlike love disappears.

Do not wait to achieve your destiny in time. Rise into it now. The real journey is not horizontal, but vertical; not geographical, but mental. The realest part of you has already arrived where you wish to end up. Time and action are the great deceivers; they separate us from the fullness already present. We believe we must wait and do, but instead we must be and know. While the ego waits and does, the spirit is calmly, firmly established in utter well-being. There are no missing pieces to import. What you seek, you already own. What you hope to achieve, you have already accomplished. What you wish to become, you already are. Your destiny was fulfilled before you set out on the epic adventure that circles back to the point of departure. Yet the journey will have been worthwhile because when you come home you will know yourself as an eternal, immortal soul. All of life is an introduction to yourself.

ACKNOWLEDGMENTS

As always, my deep gratitude to my beloved partner Dee, who stands behind me at every turn and provides a most helpful sounding board for my books and ideas that stimulate me. You are such a blessing!

I so appreciate Liz Winter, Alyssa Freeland, and Stephanie Darnell, who took the time and caring to review the book and give me their valuable opinions and suggestions.

I am again grateful to the talented and gracious Riann Bender for her immaculate interior design, and to Elena Karoumpali for her amazingly brilliant and attractive cover. What talent I am blessed to co-create with!

You, the reader, are the heart of this work. When you receive these ideas and put them into practice to make your life better, along with the lives of those you touch, this book has achieved its purpose, and my soul is fulfilled in its prayerful intention to bring healing, joy, and upliftment to the world through you.

ABOUT
THE AUTHOR

Alan Cohen, M.A., holds degrees in psychology and human organizational development. He is the author of 30 popular inspirational books, including the best-selling *A Course in Miracles Made Easy* and the award-winning *A Deep Breath of Life*. He is a contributing writer for the #1 *New York Times* best-selling series *Chicken Soup for the Soul*, and he is featured in the book *101 Top Experts Who Help Us Improve Our Lives*. His books have been translated into 32 foreign languages. Alan has taught at Montclair State College, Omega Institute for Holistic Studies, and en*theos Academy for Optimal Living. He is a featured presenter in the award-winning documentary *Finding Joe,* celebrating the teachings of Joseph Campbell. His work has been presented on CNN and Oprah.com and in *USA Today, The Washington Post*, and *Huffington Post*. His monthly column *From the Heart* is published in magazines internationally. Alan is the founder and Director of the Foundation for Holistic Life Coaching. He presents programs on themes of life mastery, spiritual development, and vision psychology. For information on Alan Cohen's books, seminars, life coach training, videos and audio recordings, visit:

www.alancohen.com

Learn More
with Alan Cohen

If you have enjoyed and benefited from *Soul and Destiny*, you may want to deepen your understanding and inspiration by participating in Alan Cohen's in-person seminars, online courses, life coach training, or online subscription programs.

Inspirational Quote for the Day—An uplifting idea e-mailed to you each day (free)

Monthly e-Newsletter—Insightful articles and announcements of upcoming events (free)

A Weekly Wave of Sanity—YouTube live presentation of inspiring ideas

The Coaching Room — Live one-to-one online coaching with Alan (free)

Live Webinars—Interactive uplifting programs on topics relevant to spirituality, self-empowerment, and holistic living

Online Courses—In-depth experiential exploration of healing, relationships, prosperity, prayer, metaphysics, and stress management

Life Coach Training—Become a certified professional holistic life coach or enhance your career and personal life with coaching skills

***A Course in Miracles* Retreat**—A residential program to empower you to master the principles and skills of this life-changing course

For information on these and other programs,
books, and recordings, visit

www.alancohen.com